Rice & Grains

KATHY KORDALIS

Rice & Grains

MORE THAN
70 DELICIOUS
& NOURISHING
RECIPES

PHOTOGRAPHY BY MOWIE KAY

RYLAND PETERS & SMALL
LONDON • NEW YORK

DEDICATION
For Matthew

Senior Designer Megan Smith
Editor Gillian Haslam
Head of Production Patricia Harrington
Art Director Leslie Harrington
Editorial Director Julia Charles
Publisher Cindy Richards

Food Stylist Kathy Kordalis
Prop Stylist Lauren Miller
Indexer Hilary Bird

Published in 2022
by Ryland Peters & Small
20–21 Jockey's Fields
London WC1R 4BW
and
341 E 116th St
New York NY 10029
www.rylandpeters.com

ISBN: 978-1-78879-429-9

10 9 8 7 6 5 4 3 2 1

Printed and bound in China.

CIP data from the Library of Congress
has been applied for.
A CIP record for this book is available
from the British Library.

NOTES

• Both British (metric) and American (imperial plus US cups) measurements
are included for your convenience; however, it is important to work with
one set of measurements and not alternate between the two within a recipe.

• Ovens should be preheated to the specified temperatures. We recommend
using an oven thermometer.

• When a recipe calls for the grated zest of citrus fruit, buy unwaxed fruit and
wash well before using. If you can only find treated fruit, scrub well in warm
soapy water before using.

Contents

Introduction

Versatile, nutritious and the true grit of any meal, rice and grains can be the main event, a great side dish and beautiful in baking. Everyone has a story about how they enjoy a gorgeous bowl of porridge or a steaming sticky rice, which toppings they prefer and what they like to serve it in – it's about comfort and nourishment. But this book will take you way beyond breakfast and rice bowls, to elegantly simple small plates that make the perfect appetizer, quick-fix larger plates for a midweek family meal, or sharing platters to help you celebrate any occasion in style with friends. You will find all this, plus some great recipes for baking with grains and making satisfying extras for your pantry such as home-made oat milk, everyday loaves and crispbreads.

The world of grains is a huge topic when you consider all the different types of rice that are consumed the world over, as well as the wealth of cereal grains and seeds that have sustained us since crops were first cultivated and plants foraged. I've focused on the most readily available grains so you can easily shop at your local convenience store, supermarket and food hall or raid your own store-cupboard at home. A little background on the origins and some basic nutritional facts is provided but, for me, the most important thing is how they taste. This is not a nutritionist's companion, my book is simply intended to inspire you to create more vibrant rice and grain dishes in your kitchen. It's a book for people who love life and good food and my recipes aim to elevate these ancient and humble ingredients in a modern and light way. Enjoy!

Rice

Rice is the second most widely cultivated grain in the world and a staple in China, India, South-east Asia, Africa and Latin America. There are thousands of varieties of rice. In the world's major rice-growing areas each paddy field will yield it's own particular strain. In the West however we classify rice by the length of its grain; a sensible classification since, as a rule, the grain length determines how it should be cooked and whether it is suitable for sweet or savoury dishes. It is always cooked before eating and also made into flour, flaked, toasted and puffed.

There are a number of ways of cooking rice. Some types, benefit from being rinsed in cold water, while others should be left to soak before cooking. Rinsing is suitable for most types of rice. It helps to remove excess starch and any dust that may have accumulated during storage. If you rinse rice which is to be in a dish where it is fried at the beginning of the recipe, be sure to drain it thoroughly first. Soaking is suitable for basmati, brown basmati, glutinous rice and sometimes white long grain, brown long grain, short grain rice and Thai fragrant (jasmine) rice. It is seldom essential but it does increase the moisture content of the grains, which means the rice will cook more quickly and will be less sticky. Soaking is particularly beneficial for basmati rice; less so for Thai fragrant (jasmine) rice, in which a slight stickiness is desired. Risotto rice, of course, must never be soaked, as this would spoil the characteristic texture. Occasionally, rice that has been soaked will be fried; if this is the case, drain it well first, as you would rinsed rice.

LONG GRAIN RICES
White Long Grain Rice; Brown Long Grain Rice; White Basmati Rice; Brown Basmati Rice; Thai Fragrant (Jasmine) Rice

This type of rice is three or four times as long as it is wide, and when cooked, the individual grains separate. Long grain rice is used for savoury dishes.

SHORT GRAIN RICES
Italian (Risotto) Rice; Spanish (Paella) Rice; Pudding Rice

Also known as round grain rice, short grain rice is used almost exclusively for making desserts. However, some short grain rices should, perhaps, be properly be described as medium grain, as their size is somewhere between pudding rice and long grain rice. These are usually used in savoury dishes requiring a creamy texture, notably Italian risotto rices such as Arborio and the short grain Valencian rice from Spain mostly known for its use in paella.

GLUTINOUS RICES
Chinese Black Rice; Japanese (Sushi) Rice

There are several types of glutinous rice that are very popular in Asian cooking. The name is misleading as the grain actually contains no gluten, but they are noted for the way they stick together after cooking. Often known as sticky rice, black and white glutinous rices are normally used to make desserts.

WILD RICES
Wild Rice; Camargue (Red) Rice

These are not really rices at all, but aquatic grasses that grow in marshy areas around the North American Great Lakes. The 'rice' was once a favourite food of the Native Americans. It is quite expensive to buy so is often served mixed with long grain rice, which also gives it a gentler and more even flavour.

SEE PAGES 10-11

Cereal Grains

Cereal grains have been cultivated throughout the world for centuries. The most popular types of grain such as rice (see page 8), wheat, oats, corn and rye come in various forms, from wholegrains to flours. They all form a hugely important part of our diet, whether eaten in bread, pasta or noodles, baked into cakes or cookies, or (ideally), enjoyed in a less processed form. In recent years, we have been enjoying a wider range of wholegrains as part of a move towards a healthier diet, whether that is rediscovering more nutritious ancient grains (such as spelt) or gluten-free alternatives to wheat (such as quinoa and amaranth).

WHEAT
Wheat Berries; Cracked Wheat; Bulgur; Wheat Flakes; Wheat Germ; Bran; Semolina

This is the largest and most important grain crop in the world and it has been cultivated since 7,000 BC. The wheat kernel comprises three parts: the bran, the germ and the endosperm. Wheat bran is the outer husk, while wheat germ is the nutritious seed from which the plant grows. Wheat Berries are the whole wheat grains with the husks removed. Cracked wheat is made from crushed wheat berries – often confused with bulgur and retains all the nutrients from whole wheat. Wheat is very important nutrionally as it is an important source of complex carbohydrates, protein, vitamins and minerals. It is most nutritious when it is unprocessed and in its whole form. It is an excellent source of dietary fibre and is rich in B vitamins and vitamin E, as well as iron, zinc and selenium.

OATS
Rolled/Old-fashioned Oats; Jumbo Oats; Oatmeal; Whole Oats; Oat Bran

The most beloved of all cereal whole grains, oats are almost never refined, which means they retain all three of its original, edible parts – the bran layer, full of fibre and B vitamins; the germ, rich in healthy oils and other nutrients; and the starchy endosperm. They also contain a heart-protective starch called beta-glucan that can help lower high cholesterol. Available rolled, flaked, as porridge (oatmeal) or oat bran, oats are warming and sustaining.

CORN (MAIZE)
Cornmeal; Polenta; Hominy; Popcorn: Grits

A staple crop in South and Central America, corn is grown in Europe, but as it needs more sunshine than wheat it grows best in the more Southerly parts, such as Italy. It is processed to produce many different products including, whole grains, flour and meal. Coarse ground cornmeal is used for polenta (see page 9), finer grinds are used for breadmaking. It is believed to be the only grain to contain vitamin A. It is also the source of some B vitamins, vitamin C and iron.

RYE
Rye Grain; Rye Flakes; Rye Flour

Rye is a hardy grain that can grow where most others fail. It is the most popular grain for bread-making in many parts of Northern and Eastern Europe, Russia and Scandinavia. It produces dark, dense and dry breads that keep well, as well as crispbreads. Rye is a good source of vitamin E and some B vitamins, as well as protein, calcium, iron, phosphorus and potassium, and is high in fibre.

SEE PAGES 12–13

Types of Rice

WHITE LONG GRAIN RICE

This is the most commonly available white rice. It has been fully milled, in other words, all of the bran and outer coating have been removed. The grains are white and slightly shiny. It doesn't have the flavour of basmati or Thai fragrant, rice, but remains a good all-rounder and a firm favourite.

BROWN LONG GRAIN RICE

Sometimes called 'whole rice', this is the rice equivalent of wholemeal (whole-wheat) bread, complete with the bran. It has an almost nutty flavour.

ITALIAN (RISOTTO) RICE

A large quantity and variety of rice is produced in Italy. Most is grown in the Po Valley. The rice is classified by size, ranging from the shortest, *ordinario*, to *superfino*. Most of the risotto rices are *fino* and *superfino* varieties. Arborio is one of the best-known Italian risotto rices. Unlike the finer risotto rices such as carnaroli, arborio has a comparatively large, plump grain. Risotto rice is available both white and brown.

SPANISH (PAELLA) RICE

Rice is grown extensively in Spain, particularly in the swampy regions outside Valencia. The most common is a medium short grain variety with a slightly sticky consistency when cooked and is used for paella. Bomba is a plump paella rice which, like Italian risotto rice, absorbs liquid. Calasperra is another top-quality short grain Spanish variety.

PUDDING RICE

This is a short grain white rice, particularly suitable for slow-cooked milky puddings as the grains swell and absorb a lot of liquid The rice becomes soft and sticky, giving a deliciously smooth and creamy texture.

CAMARGUE (RED) RICE

Often referred to as 'red rice', this nutty rice is grown in the Camargue region of France. It came about as a result of cross-pollination between local white rice and an indigenous wild red rice. Uncooked it is a reddish-brown, much like brown rice, however as it cooks the red intensifies.

CHINESE BLACK RICE

Also known as 'forbidden rice', this highly-prized variety of black long-grain rice is grown in China. Once cooked, it turns a purple colour and develops a stickiness and a pleasing nutty-sweet taste.

WHITE LONG GRAIN RICE

CHINESE BLACK RICE

BROWN ITALIAN (RISOTTO) RICE

PUDDING RICE

BROWN BASMATI RICE

THAI FRAGRANT (JASMINE) RICE

WHITE ITALIAN RISOTTO RICE (ARBORIO)

THAI FRAGRANT (JASMINE) RICE

Grown in Thailand and Vietnam, this rice has a fragrant, almost milky aroma. It is widely used in South-East Asian cooking and goes well with spicy dishes typical of the region. It is highly prized and commonly reserved for feasts and celebrations, rather than for everyday meals. It cooks quickly and has a slightly sticky texture.

JAPANESE (SUSHI) RICE

Japanese rice refers to short- and medium-grained rices of the type eaten in Japan. It is more starchy and round than the long-grain varieties, which don't hold together well enough to support ingredients. It's unique qualities make it ideal for use in sushi-making, so many stores now sell varieties labelled 'sushi' rice.

WHITE BASMATI RICE

This comes mainly from the Punjab region of India, adjacent parts of Pakistan and the foothills of the Himalayas. The Hindi word basmati means 'the fragrant one'. The grains are long and slender and during cooking become even longer, which partly accounts for its wonderful texture. It is the essential rice for biryani.

BROWN BASMATI RICE

Like brown long grain rice, brown basmati comes with the bran but without the husk, has all the flavour of white basmati but with the added texture of brown rice.

WILD RICE

Though wild rice mimics conventionally grown rice in many ways, it isn't actually a true rice – it's an aquatic grass with an edible grain. Wild rice tends to be longer, has a more nutty, earthy flavour and the hull is thicker and more rigid. It takes much longer to prepare and has a very strong distinctive flavour. Wild rice is often mixed with other long-grain rice to make for a more even and gentler flavour, as well as a more affordable product.

BROWN LONG GRAIN RICE

WILD RICE MIX

BASMATI RICE

WILD RICE

CARMARGUE (RED) RICE

SPANISH (PAELLA) RICE

JAPANESE (SUSHI) RICE

Grains & Grain Products

POLENTA

Polenta (cornmeal) has its roots in the peasant cuisine of Northern Italy. It's made by grinding corn (see page 9), into meal. It can be cooked to be creamy and thick, or allowed to set and sliced, or can be used in place of breadcrumbs when frying.

JUMBO OATS

Made by rolling the whole oat grain. See Oats, page 9.

PINHEAD OATMEAL

The largest and coarsest oatmeal. See Oats, page 9.

FREEKEH

Freekeh is made from young durum wheat (see Wheat, page 9) which is roasted or smoked then polished to remove the shells. The green whole grains (shown here) are then cracked to varying degrees of coarseness. It is similar in texture to bulgur wheat and has a rich, nutty, smoky flavour.

RYE GRAIN

Rye, in its unprocessed form. See Rye, page 9.

BARLEY

Believed to be the oldest cultivated grain, barley is still a key part of the everyday diet in Eastern Europe, the Middle East and Asia. This nutty, high-fibre grain is sold in two forms, hulled and pearled (shown here). Hulled barley undergoes minimal processing to remove only the inedible outer shell, leaving the bran and germ intact. Enjoy it in soups and stews, or as an alternative to rice for a risotto.

BUCKWHEAT

In spite of its name, buckwheat is not actually a type of wheat. Buckwheat groats (shown here) have a nutty, earthy flavour and are a staple food in Eastern Europe and Russia. Buckwheat flour is used to make Japanese soba noodles, while buckwheat pancakes (gallettes) are eaten in France.

MILLET

Millet is a highly nutritious grain that once rivalled barley as the main food of Europe. It remains a staple ingredient in many parts of the work. Its mild flavour goes well with spicy curries.

POLENTA

WHOLE GRAIN FREEKAH

RYE GRAIN

JUMBO OATS

PINHEAD OATMEAL

QUINOA

Hailed as a supergrain, quinoa was known as 'the mother grain' by the inca, who grew it for hundreds of years, high up in the Andes. The tiny, bead-shaped grains are most commonly white and red, although available in black (shown here) or purple. It is also available in flake form.

SPELT

This is one of the most ancient cultivated crops. Spelt grains (shown here) look similar to wheat and once ground the flour can be substituted for wheat flour in bread. It has a higher nutritional content than wheat.

BULGUR

This tasty grain is made from whole wheatberries (see Wheat, page 9), but unlike cracked wheat, the berries are cooked, the bran removed and they are dried and crushed. It is light and nutty and very easy to cook.

AMARANTH

Native to Mexico, amaranth can be eaten as a vegetable (the leaves are similar to spinach) or as a grain. Once harvested, the tiny amaranth seeds (shown here) are revealed to be a nearly uniform shade of pale cream, and retain a little texture once cooked. They can be used for porridges and pilafs, and are also ground into flour for gluten-free baking.

SPELT GRAIN

PEARL BARLEY

BUCKWHEAT GROATS

MILLET

BULGUR

AMARANTH SEED

BLACK QUINOA

Breakfasts

Five-grain granola

The perfect start to any day! This granola is just as delicious whether served with a plant-based or a dairy yogurt. The combination of syrups, coconut dried fruit and all the grains make this a light, layered-in-flavour breakfast or anytime snack.

Preheat the oven to 180°C (350°F) Gas 4. Line several baking sheets with parchment paper.

Mix together oats and flakes, nuts, puffed rice, seeds and cinnamon in a bowl. Warm the maple syrup and rice syrup in a pan over a low heat, then add the oil and stir to mix. Pour over the oat mixture and stir to coat, then spread the mixture on the lined baking sheets. Bake in the preheated oven for 15–20 minutes, stirring occasionally, until crisp and golden. Allow to cool on the baking sheets. Granola will keep in an airtight container for 2 weeks.

Try the granola with tropical fruit salad with lemongrass and passion-fruit, rice malt syrup and coconut yogurt.

100 g/1 cup each rolled/old-fashioned oats, spelt flakes, quinoa flakes and rye flakes

200 g/1½ cups mixed nuts

60 g/2½ cups puffed rice

100 g/generous ⅔ cups mixed sunflower seeds and pumpkin seeds

2 teaspoons ground cinnamon

200 ml/scant 1 cup maple syrup

100 ml/scant ½ cup rice syrup

50 g/2 oz. coconut oil

SERVES 8–10

Grainy porridge

This earthy porridge base has a wonderfully deep flavour. See page 19 for three ways to make your porridge using this dry base.

Working in batches, toast the oats, spelt flakes and rye flakes in a large, dry frying pan/skillet for 5 minutes until golden, then leave to cool and store in an airtight container.

When you want to eat it, simply combine 50 g/½ cup of the porridge mixture in a saucepan with 300 ml/1¼ cups milk or water. Cook for 5 minutes, stirring occasionally.

200 g/2 cups rolled/old-fashioned oats

200 g/2 cups spelt flakes

200 g/2 cups rye flakes

SERVES 8–10

Grainy porridge three ways

Here are three elegant ways to eat your grainy porridge. The overnight oats combine nut milk with nuts and cinnamon and finish with a nut butter and freshly grated apple for some zing. The earth bowl is nutty and nourishing with dates, spices, dried pineapple and bee pollen. The berries and rose water pair for a beautiful porridge for a start to the day fit for a queen. Note: each of these recipes serves 1 and requires 50 g/½ cup of Grainy Porridge (see page 16).

OVERNIGHT NO-COOK PORRIDGE

The night before serving, stir the cinnamon and almond milk into your grainy porridge with a pinch of salt.

The next day, loosen with a little more water if needed. Top with the yogurt, dried fruit and nuts, apple, a drizzle of honey and the nut butter.

EARTH BOWL PORRIDGE

Put the grainy porridge into a saucepan with the cashew milk and stir. Add the dates, nuts, chia seeds and cocoa powder and cook for 5 minutes, stirring occasionally.

Top with the extra chopped dates, dried pineapple, rice malt syrup and dried pineapple.

BERRIES & ROSE PORRIDGE

Put the grainy porridge into a saucepan with the oat milk, cinnamon and honey. Cook gently for 5 minutes, stirring, until the oats are creamy and cooked. Tip in the frozen berries and cook for 2 minutes or until warmed through. Stir through the cashew butter, coconut yogurt, a few drops of rose water, then spoon into a serving bowl and top with fresh berries and a few rose petals, if using.

---

50 g/½ cup Grainy Porridge (see page 16)

OVERNIGHT NO-COOK PORRIDGE

¼ teaspoon ground cinnamon

100 ml/scant ½ cup almond milk

a pinch of salt

2 tablespoons plant-based yogurt

50 g/⅓ cup mixed dried fruit and nuts

1 apple, grated, plus extra to finish

a drizzle of honey

½ tablespoon nut butter

EARTH BOWL PORRIDGE

300 ml/1¼ cups cashew milk

30 g/1 oz. chopped dates (plus extra to finish)

30 g/scant ¼ cup mixed nuts, chopped

2 tablespoons chia seeds

½ teaspoon cinnamon

½ teaspoon raw cocoa powder

2 dried pineapple rings, roughly chopped

1–2 tablespoons rice malt syrup

1 teaspoon bee pollen

BERRIES & ROSE PORRIDGE

250 ml/1 cup Simple Oat Milk (see page 23)

½ teaspoon ground cinnamon

1–2 teaspoons honey (or to taste)

100 g/3½ oz. frozen berries

2 tablespoons cashew butter

1–2 tablespoons coconut yogurt

a few drops of rose water

a handful of fresh berries

a few edible rose petals (optional)

SERVES 1

Almond amaranth break-feast bowl with green tea & ginger-poached fruit

Amaranth is a gluten-free grain but, unlike other grains such as rice and quinoa, it does not puff up when cooked. Instead, after cooking the amaranth seeds remain tiny and they become soft and tender, yet maintain a bit of a crunch. Amaranth has a delicate nutty flavour and is great as a porridge alternative. The flavours in this recipe are all delicate, but when they come together they create a really special breakfast or brunch bowl.

Start by rinsing the amaranth in a sieve/strainer under cold running water to remove the saponins (natural compounds that leave a slightly bitter taste). Tip the amaranth into bowl and add the almonds, pistachios, almond milk and 150 ml/⅔ cup water, cover and refrigerate overnight.

The apricots can be poached in advance. Place all the ingredients in a saucepan with 200 ml/scant 1 cup water and simmer for 5–10 minutes (depending on how ripe the apricots are – you need them to have a little bite and not be too soft). Allow to cool and store in the fridge. Bring to room temperature before serving.

The next morning, pour the contents of the amaranth bowl into a saucepan and bring to the boil, then turn down the heat, cover the pan and cook for 10–15 minutes until the grains are tender and the liquid has been absorbed. Stir in the chia seeds. Stir through the coconut cream for a porridge consistency.

Divide the amaranth mixture between 4 bowls and finish with the poached apricots and some of the poaching liquid to serve.

170 g/scant 1 cup amaranth

70 g/generous ½ cup almonds and pistachios, roughly chopped

500 ml/2 cups almond milk

3 tablespoons chia seeds

3 tablespoon coconut cream, plus extra for serving

GREEN TEA & GINGER-POACHED APRICOTS

4 apricots, halved and stoned/pitted

1 thumb-sized piece of fresh ginger, peeled and sliced

50 g/¼ cup light soft brown sugar

1 green tea bag

SERVES 4

Simple oat milk

It is so satisfying to make oat milk from scratch. More delicious than store-bought options and with no added extras, it's perfect for smoothies and porridge bowls or add a dash to your coffee.

200 g/2 cups rolled/
  old-fashioned oats
1 teaspoon sea salt

MAKES 1.5 LITRES/QUARTS

Place the oats in a bowl and cover with water until submerged. Cover and leave overnight in a cool place. Sieve/strain the mixture, discarding the water, and rinse under cold running water for a few seconds.

Place the soaked oats in a food processor, sprinkle over the sea salt and cover with 1.5 litres/quarts of cold water. Blend for 2–4 minutes until completely smooth and there are no oats visible.

Line a sieve/strainer with muslin/cheesecloth and place over a bowl. Pour in the oat milk and leave to strain for 1 hour. Every once in a while, use a spoon to scrape the bottom of the cloth to disperse some of the sediment. When most of the liquid is in the bowl, gather the sides of the muslin/cheesecloth together and squeeze tightly with both hands to extract the last of the milk. Discard the solids.

This oat milk keeps for 2–3 days in the fridge. Shake well before use.

Oat, blueberry &
peanut smoothie

A very simple but stunning combination – so nourishing for breakfast on-the-go. You can add any nut butter but I love peanut, combined with banana, blueberries and oats and sometimes add a scoop of vanilla or chocolate protein powder.

1 banana
100 g/¾ cup blueberries
1 tablespoon rolled/
  old-fashioned oats
150 ml/⅔ cup Simple Oat Milk
  (see above)
1 tablespoon peanut butter
1 teaspoon maple syrup
a handful of ice cubes

SERVES 1

Put all the ingredients in a blender and whizz for 1 minute until smooth. Serve chilled.

Blueberry barley streusel muffins

Barley flour is just plain amazing in baking. Although muffins may seem simple, they are very easy to get wrong, ending up dry and stodgy. The barley flour in this recipes gives you a gentle, slightly nutty and not super-sweet muffin. Using the fruit frozen helps it to stay intact during the baking process, while the streusel topping keeps the muffins moist for a few days.

Preheat the oven to 180°C (350°F) Gas 4. Line a 12-hole muffin pan with paper cases.

To prepare the streusel topping, mix together the sugar, barley flour and cinnamon in a small bowl. Add the butter and bring the mixture together gently, being careful not to overmix. Set aside.

In a large bowl, whisk the barley flour, baking powder, bicarbonate of soda/baking soda and salt together. Set aside. In a medium bowl, whisk the melted butter with the sugar, then add the eggs, milk, yogurt and vanilla paste and mix again.

Add the wet ingredients to the dry ingredients and gently stir using a rubber spatula until almost combined. Fold in the blueberries until just combined.

Divide the batter between the 12 paper cases, filling all the way to the top. Sprinkle with the streusel topping.

Bake on the middle shelf of the preheated oven for 12 minutes, then rotate the pan and bake for 12 minutes more, until the muffins are a rich golden colour and a toothpick inserted in the centre of one comes out clean.

These muffins will keep for 2 days in an airtight container.

300 g/2 cups barley flour

1 tablespoon baking powder

1 teaspoon bicarbonate of soda/baking soda

a pinch of salt

130 g/1 stick plus 1 tablespoon unsalted butter, melted and cooled

200 g/1 cup light soft brown sugar

2 large/US extra-large eggs

250 g/scant 1¼ cups Greek yogurt

1 teaspoon vanilla paste

200 g/generous 1 cup frozen blueberries

STREUSEL TOPPING

100 g/scant ½ cup demerara/raw sugar

80 g/generous ½ cup barley flour

a pinch of ground cinnamon

70 g/5 tablespoons cold unsalted butter

MAKES 12

Simple seeded rye loaf

This is my Sunday baking staple. I make a loaf every Sunday and toast it, make it into sandwiches and dip it in olive oil – the list goes on. When it's down to its last few chunks I roast it with a few tomatoes, drizzled with olive oil, balsamic vinegar, garlic, a little chopped chilli/chile, some feta and maybe a fried egg. Every last morsel is consumed. See photo on page 28.

350 g/2½ cups strong wholemeal/whole-wheat flour

150 g/heaping 1 cup dark rye flour

2 teaspoons salt

7 g/2 teaspoons instant/fast-action dried yeast

70 g/½ cup linseeds/flaxseeds (reserve some for topping)

70 g/½ cup pumpkin seeds (reserve some for topping)

70 g/½ cup sunflower seeds (reserve some for topping)

1 teaspoon caraway seeds

3 teaspoons poppyseeds (reserve some for topping)

80 ml/⅓ cup black treacle/molasses

300 ml/1¼ cups water

MAKES 1 LOAF

Mix the flours, salt, yeast and seeds in a large bowl. Add the black treacle/molasses and water, then mix well. If the dough seems a little stiff, add 1 tablespoon or more extra water. Mix well, then put on a lightly floured work surface and gently knead the dough for 7 minutes. Put it back into a lightly oiled bowl and allow to rise in a warm place for about 2 hours until doubled in size.

Line a baking sheet with parchment paper.

Tip the dough onto a lightly floured work surface and knock back, then gently mould the dough into a ball. Roll the dough in the reserved seeds and place on the lined baking sheet to prove for a further hour until doubled in size.

Preheat the oven to 220°C (425°F) Gas 7 and put a roasting pan in the bottom. Boil a kettle of water.

Place the loaf in the preheated oven, then – working very quickly – half-fill the roasting pan with boiling water. Bake for about 35 minutes until the loaf is well browned on top and the base sounds fairly hollow when tapped. Allow to cool on a rack before slicing.

Oat bread
with spiced butter

Slightly earthy and slightly nutty, this oat bread is just delicious with a hunk of Cheddar or with this spiced butter. It is best eaten on the day of baking, although the leftover oat bread makes great French toast with berries and honey. Or on the day of baking, slice and freeze, ready to toast. See photo on page 29.

For the oat bread, in a large mixing bowl, or in the bowl of a stand mixer, mix together all of the ingredients to form a rough dough. Knead the dough, by hand or in the mixer, until it's springy but still soft, about 5–7 minutes. The dough may feel quite sticky at the beginning, but don't add any extra liquid as it will dry out. Place the dough in a lightly greased bowl, cover and allow it to rise at room temperature for 1 hour.

Meanwhile, whip the butter with the spices, honey and salt and place into a small bowl, ready to serve with the bread.

Preheat the oven to 180°C (350°F) Gas 4. Lightly oil a 2-lb loaf pan.

Transfer the dough to a lightly oiled surface. Flatten the dough into a rectangle. Fold the top down to the centre, pressing it firmly with the heel of your hand to seal. Pull the upper left and right corners into the centre, pressing to seal. Repeat the first step three or four more times, until you've created a log. Tuck the ends under slightly, and turn the log over so its seam is on the bottom and place into the loaf pan,. Leave it covered for a further 30 minutes or until doubled in size.

Brush the loaf with the egg wash and scatter with the oats. Bake the bread in the preheated oven for 35–40 minutes, until it's golden brown. If the bread appears to be browning too quickly, cover it lightly with foil for the final 10 minutes of baking. It's ready when the base sounds hollow when tapped. Allow to cool for 20 minutes before slicing and serving with the spiced butter or a chunk of Cheddar.

260 g/scant 2 cups strong white bread flour

100 g/¾ cup strong wholemeal/whole-wheat bread flour

50 g/⅓ cup fine oatmeal

100 g/1 cup rolled/old-fashioned oats, plus extra to finish

30 g/2 tablespoons butter, softened

1 teaspoon sea salt

2 tablespoons black treacle/molasses

7 g/2 teaspoons instant/fast-action dried yeast

270 ml/1 cup plus 2 tablespoons lukewarm milk

1 egg, beaten, for the egg wash

SPICED BUTTER

150 g/1¼ sticks butter, at room temperature

1 teaspoon ground cinnamon

½ teaspoon ground allspice

1 teaspoon ground cardamom

2 teaspoons honey

a pinch of salt

MAKES 1 LOAF

Pear, rooibos,
date & spelt loaf

This is a gentle sweet loaf that is great for breakfast or brunch, or in fact any time of day. Infuse the dates with rooibos as its honeyed vanilla flavour pairs well with the pear and spelt for a moist loaf.

Preheat the oven to 160°C (325°F) Gas 3. Line the base and long sides of a 900-g/2-lb loaf pan with parchment paper, buttering the pan and paper.

In a bowl add the rooibos tea to the dates and the bicarbonate of soda/baking soda. Allow to sit and brew for 10 minutes.

Meanwhile, in a stand mixer mix the butter and sugar until light and fluffy. In a separate bowl mix the spelt flour, baking powder and cardamom, if using, and set aside. Gradually add the beaten eggs little by little into the butter and sugar, allowing it to mix in well. Turn off the machine and add the flour, the soaked and drained dates (discarding the soaking liquid) and the grated pears. Stir in by hand, making sure you do not over mix.

Pour the batter into the prepared loaf pan, top with the sliced reserved pear and bake in the preheated oven for around 45 minutes or until baked through and a skewer inserted into the centre comes out clean. Brush the top of the loaf and the pears with maple syrup and leave to cool in the pan for 15 minutes, then transfer to a wire rack to cool completely for a further 15 minutes before serving.

100 ml/scant ½ cup infused rooibos tea

150 g/5½ oz. dates, roughly chopped

1 teaspoon bicarbonate of soda/baking soda

180 g/1½ sticks butter, plus extra for greasing

100 g/½ cup raw cane/rapadura sugar

250 g/scant 2 cups wholemeal/whole-wheat spelt flour

1½ teaspoons baking powder

½ teaspoon ground cardamom (optional)

3 eggs, beaten

2 grated pears, plus 1 sliced on a mandoline to decorate

maple syrup, for brushing

MAKES 1 LOAF

Savoury breakfast tart with spelt shortcrust

This is a very versatile pastry as it can be used for sweet or savoury tarts. For sweet tarts, omit the salt. This filling is a real crowd-pleaser and can be eaten at any time of day.

To make the pastry, place the butter, spelt flour, walnuts and salt into a food processor and blitz until this mixture resembles fine breadcrumbs (alternatively, do it by hand in a bowl). Stir in enough of the water to bring the pastry together into a soft dough. Form a ball, cover with clingfilm/plastic wrap and chill in the fridge for 30 minutes.

Meanwhile, to prepare the filling, heat a frying pan/skillet on a medium-high heat, add the olive oil and the chopped shallots and cook until caramelized, turning every few minutes. Add the thyme sprigs and the spinach and heat until it has wilted. Set aside until ready to use. In a separate bowl place the eggs, crème fraîche or sour cream, season with salt and pepper and mix. Set aside until ready to use.

Preheat the oven to 200°C (400°F) Gas 6.

Take the pastry out of the fridge. Dust the work surface with flour, then roll out the pastry into a circle 5 cm/2 inches larger than your dish and lift it into the tart pan. Leave an overhang of pastry around the sides of the pan. Prick the base of the pastry case all over with a fork. Line the tart pan with parchment paper and fill with ceramic baking beans or dried pulses. Bake in the preheated oven for about 15 minutes or until the pastry is firm, then remove the beans and paper and cook for a further 5 minutes, until golden brown.

Turn the oven down to 160°C (325°F) Gas 3.

Place the shallot and spinach mixture in the base of the tart case, add the semi-dried tomatoes, then pour in the egg and crème fraîche mixture. Lay the pancetta slices randomly, sprinkle over the Parmesan and bake for 30 minutes or until the filling has set. Remove from the oven, allow to cool before removing from the pan, sprinkle with thyme, if using, and serve.

100 g/7 tablespoons butter
200 g/1¾ cups wholemeal/whole-wheat spelt flour
50 g/⅓ cup walnuts
a pinch of salt
8–9 tablespoons cold water
butter, for greasing
flour, for dusting

FILLING
2 tablespoons olive oil
3 shallots, chopped
4 sprigs of lemon thyme
100 g/3½ oz. baby spinach
5 eggs, beaten
2 tablespoons crème fraîche or sour cream
100 g/3½ oz. semi-dried tomatoes, store-bought
90 g/3 oz. thinly sliced pancetta
20 g/¼ cup grated Parmesan
salt and freshly ground black pepper
fresh thyme, leaves stripped, to garnish (optional)

20-cm/8-inch tart pan

SERVES 6

Savoury rice porridge

Slow-cooked rice in chicken stock, cooked long enough for the rice to break down and form a warm hug in a bowl – a version of this is eaten all over Asia for breakfast or, for a comforting meal. It is intended to be very plain, with some simple garnishes. My favourite type of rice to use for this is brown rice and I absolutely love it with a dollop of chilli-black bean sauce and a slice of bacon for a super-comforting meal full of goodness.

Place the stock, rice, ginger and 2.25 litres/quarts water in a large saucepan and bring to a simmer over medium-high heat.

Reduce the heat to low, half-cover with a lid and simmer, stirring occasionally, until the mixture reaches a porridge consistency (this will take 1¼–1½ hours). Season to taste with sea salt and coarsely ground white pepper.

Serve hot, topped with your choice of thinly sliced spring onion/scallion, grated fresh ginger, chilli-black bean sauce, soy sauce, sesame seeds and/or pan-fried crispy bacon.

750 ml/3 cups chicken stock

350 g/1¾ cups brown rice

30 g/1 oz. fresh ginger, thinly sliced plus extra, finely grated, to serve

2 tablespoons vegetable oil

sea salt and coarsely ground white pepper

TO SERVE (ALL OPTIONAL)

thinly sliced spring onion/scallion

grated fresh ginger

chilli-black bean sauce

soy sauce

sesame seeds

thick bacon, pan-fried with the pan juices

SERVES 2

Small Plates

Toasted mixed grains
with lemon labne

Absolute heaven on a plate! It's hard to know where to begin – the toasted grains for added flavour, the lemony creamy home-made labne, finished with sweet and sour pomegranate molasses. Pre-toasting the grains adds another element to this perfect dish.

Start the lemon labne the night before. Combine the yogurt, lemon zest and juice, garlic, salt and freshly ground black pepper (to taste) in a bowl, then transfer to a sieve/strainer lined with muslin/cheesecloth, place over a bowl to catch the liquid and refrigerate overnight to drain.

Dry-roast the spelt and faro in a frying pan/skillet for 1–2 minutes until nutty and fragrant. Tip the grains into a saucepan, cover with boiling water and simmer for 15–20 minutes until tender, then drain and refresh under cold running water. Drain well and transfer to a large bowl. Meanwhile, cook the quinoa in a pan of boiling salted water for 4–5 minutes, add the bulgur, cook for another minute, drain well and refresh under cold running water. Drain well and add to spelt mixture.

Make the pomegranate dressing directly in the serving bowl by whisking all the ingredients together, then season to taste. In the same dish add the green lentils, pistachios, dried apricots, red onion and all the cooked grains, season to taste and toss to combine. Gently mix through all the micro herbs and greens.

To serve, on small plates place a dollop of labne to the side and sprinkle with za'atar. Add some of the grainy mix, top with pomegranate seeds, then drizzle with olive oil.

50 g/⅓ cup spelt grain

50 g/⅓ cup faro

60 g/⅓ cup quinoa grains

60 g/⅓ cup bulgur

400-g/14-oz. can green lentils, drained

80 g/⅔ cup pistachios, coarsely chopped

75 g/½ cup dried apricots, coarsely chopped

1 red onion, thinly sliced

150 g/5½ oz. mixed micro herbs and leaves

LEMON LABNE

500 g/2¼ cups Greek yogurt

grated zest and freshly squeezed juice of 1 lemon

1 garlic clove, crushed

1½ teaspoons salt

freshly ground black pepper

POMEGRANATE DRESSING

80 ml/⅓ cup extra-virgin olive oil

2 tablespoons red wine vinegar

freshly squeezed juice of 1 lemon

2 tablespoons pomegranate molasses

½ pomegranate, seeds only

a pinch of za'atar

sea salt and freshly ground black pepper

TO SERVE

1 tablespoon za'atar

½ pomegranate, seeds only

olive oil, to drizzle

SERVES 4–6

Grainy falafel with coriander-feta pesto

Traditionally, falafel are made with ground chickpeas and/or broad/fava beans. To achieve a crispy outside and a moist inside it is best to use dried chickpeas that have been soaked overnight. This recipe sticks to chickpeas, with the addition of rye flakes and millet – both are ancient grains and are high in fibre and protein and provide an extra little kick of nutrition. Serve alongside the coriander/cilantro-feta pesto for the perfect snack.

Drain the chickpeas, discarding the soaking liquid, and process in a food processor with the rye flakes, millet, shallots, green chilli/chile, garlic, spices and herbs until a fine paste forms. Stir through the flour and bicarbonate of soda/baking soda, and season to taste. Roll the mixture into about 12 walnut-sized oval balls. Place on a baking sheet lined with parchment paper and refrigerate until chilled.

Meanwhile, to make the pesto, in a food processor blitz the coriander/cilantro, walnuts and feta into a chunky mixture, then add the olive oil. Mix in the oil, keeping the texture of the pesto chunky.

Fill a medium saucepan with vegetable oil to a depth of 7.5 cm/3 inches. Heat the oil over a medium-high heat until it bubbles softly. Using a slotted spoon, carefully lower the falafel patties into the oil and let them fry for about 3–5 minutes or so until crispy and medium brown on the outside. Avoid overcrowding the falafel in the saucepan and fry them in batches if necessary. Drain on paper towels.

Serve the falafel warm or at room temperature, plated with some coriander/cilantro-feta pesto, roasted red (bell) pepper (if liked) and wedges of lime for squeezing.

250 g/1½ cups dried chickpeas, soaked overnight in cold water

40 g/scant ½ cup rye flakes, plus 3 tablespoons to finish

60 g/scant ⅓ cup millet, cooked and cooled

2 shallots, chopped

1 green chilli/chile, finely chopped

1 garlic clove, crushed

1 teaspoon each ground coriander, cumin and smoked paprika

½ teaspoon ground cinnamon

½ teaspoon dried chilli/hot red pepper flakes

30 g/1 oz. coarsely chopped mixed flat-leaf parsley and coriander/cilantro

2 tablespoons rye flour

1 teaspoon bicarbonate of soda/baking soda

sea salt and freshly ground black pepper

vegetable oil, for deep-frying

lime wedges, to serve

1 jar of roasted red (bell) peppers, chopped, to serve (optional)

CORIANDER/CILANTRO-FETA PESTO

60 g/3½ cups coriander/cilantro, chopped

50 g/⅓ cup walnuts, chopped

100 g/3½ oz. feta, crumbled

80 ml/⅓ cup olive oil

SERVES 4–6

Buckwheat blinis with smoked salmon & chive sauce

These are based on a Russian blini recipe that is perfect served with some gravlax or plain smoked salmon, whatever you prefer. In fact, blinis have a long history in Slavic cuisines. Once you have made them at home, you will truly never buy shop-bought blinis again. The buckwheat flour gives them a lovely colour and a slightly nutty, toasty flavour.

To make the blinis, put the flour, baking powder and a pinch of salt if used into a bowl, stir to combine and sift into a mixing bowl. Add the egg and half the milk and beat into a smooth paste. Beat in the remaining milk. Put a little oil into a large frying pan/skillet, roll it around to cover the surface and heat until the pan is nice and hot. Drop teaspoonfuls of batter onto the pan to make small blinis. When bubbles appear on the surface of the blinis and the base is golden, turn them over and cook the other side until golden. Transfer the cooked blinis to a cooling rack. Repeat with the remaining batter.

To make the chive sauce, mix all the ingredients together in a bowl and check for seasoning.

Serve the blinis with smoked salmon or gravlax, chive sauce and extra lemon wedges for squeezing.

your preferred smoked salmon/lox or gravlax, to serve (allow 100–150 g/ 4–6 oz. per person)

BLINIS (MAKES 18–20)

75 g/½ cup buckwheat flour

1 teaspoon baking powder

1 egg

150 ml/⅔ cup milk

salt

2 tablespoons of oil, for frying

lemon wedges, to serve

CHIVE SAUCE

200 g/7 oz. crème fraîche

finely grated zest and freshly squeezed juice of 1 lemon

20 g/¾ oz. chives, finely chopped and chive flowers

1 teaspoon horseradish, or to taste

SERVES 4–6

Corn & quinoa fritters with crispy bacon & beetroot yogurt

Delicious little rosti-style fritters can be rustled up with almost any leftover vegetables that you have – here I've used sweetcorn/corn, courgettes/zucchini and carrots, and added crispy quinoa flakes into the mix. These are best served straight from the pan while still hot, and I enjoy them with crispy bacon (but this is optional) and a garlicky yogurt and beet dip.

Start by removing the excess moisture from the grated courgettes/zucchini by wrapping them in muslin/cheesecloth and squeezing out excess moisture. Combine the courgette/zucchini, carrots, corn, coriander/cilantro, spring onions/scallions, ground coriander and green chilli/chile in a bowl.

Place chickpea flour, quinoa, eggs and 150 ml/⅔ cup water in a bowl. Whisk to combine. Season with salt and pepper. Pour the batter into the bow of vegetables and mix well to combine, then set aside for 30 minutes.

Meanwhile, preheat the oven to 180°C (350°F) Gas 4. Lay the bacon slices in a single layer on a baking sheet (do not let them overlap or they will stick together). Bake until the bacon is crispy – about 20 minutes, depending on its thickness. Keep warm.

Make the beetroot/beet yogurt by mixing all the ingredients in a bowl, season well and taste.

Heat the olive oil in a frying pan/skillet over a medium heat. Add 1 heaped tablespoon/¼ cup measures of fritter mixture to the pan. Cook for 4 minutes on each side and drain on paper towels. Repeat with the remaining mixture and keep warm.

Serve the fritters with the bacon and beetroot/beet yogurt and topped with coriander/cilantro leaves and lime wedges. Chilli/chili jam and chopped spring onions/scallions also go well.

2 courgettes/zucchini, grated (about 250 g/9 oz.)

2 carrots, grated (approx. 200 g/7 oz.)

2 corn cobs, kernels removed (about 200 g/7 oz.)

½ bunch coriander/cilantro, finely chopped

1 bunch spring onions/scallions, finely chopped

1 teaspoon ground coriander

1 green chilli/chile, finely chopped

100 g/1 cup chickpea flour

190 g/2 cups quinoa flakes

4 eggs, lightly beaten

180 g/6½ oz. streaky/fatty bacon

3 tablespoons olive oil

sea salt and freshly ground black pepper

BEETROOT/BEET YOGURT

200 g/scant 1 cup Greek yogurt

1 garlic clove, crushed

1 raw beetroot/beet, peeled and grated

1 teaspoon ground coriander

freshly squeezed juice of 1 lime

1 tablespoon olive oil

TO SERVE

coriander/cilantro leaves

lime wedges

SERVES 4–6

Spanish-style mini stuffed vegetables

Paella rice melds with chorizo and saffron to make a tasty filling with a sunny Spanish twist for these stuffed vegetables. The addition of the sherry vinegar and sugar finishes them with a sweet and sour twist.

Slice off the top of the tomatoes (save the sliced-off pieces as they will form 'lids') and scoop out the insides, placing them in a bowl. Do the same with the insides of the courgettes/zucchini and aubergines/eggplants. Mash the filling and set aside. Halve the (bell) peppers and discard the seeds. Sit the vegetables snugly in a casserole dish, cut-side up.

Preheat the oven to 200°C (400°F) Gas 6.

Heat a sauté pan to medium, add 2 tablespoons of the olive oil and the chorizo to the pan. Gently fry until golden and caramelized, then remove from the pan and set aside. In the same pan add the shallots and cook for 10–12 minutes until caramelized, then add the garlic and cook for a further few minutes. Add the rice and coat well in the oil for a few minutes. Add the reserved vegetable filling, a pinch of saffron and the vegetable stock and cook, stirring gently, for 10 minutes. Add the chorizo mixture and stir through. Use this mixture to stuff the vegetables.

Drizzle the vinegar over the stuffed vegetables, then the remaining 4 tablespoons of olive oil, and season with pinches of sugar, salt and ground black pepper. Replace the lids on the vegetables and cover the dish with foil.

Bake in the preheated oven for 30 minutes, until the vegetables are tender and collapsing a little. Remove, uncover and cook for a further 10 minutes. Leave the vegetables to cool slightly, then scatter with parsley and spoon onto plates, scooping out any extra juices for the pan. Serve with padrón peppers and crusty bread for mopping up the juices.

4 tomatoes, 4 round courgettes/zucchini or squashes, 4 mini aubergines/eggplants, 4 mini (bell) peppers

6 tablespoons olive oil

I chorizo ring, finely chopped

3 shallots, finely chopped

3 garlic cloves, crushed

200 g/generous I cup paella rice

a pinch of saffron

200 ml/scant I cup vegetable stock

4 tablespoons sherry vinegar

a pinch of caster/granulated sugar

sea salt and freshly ground black pepper

20 g/¾ oz. flat-leaf parsley, leaves picked, or salad leaves, to serve

padrón peppers, to serve (optional)

crusty bread, to serve

SERVES 4–6

Squid ink risotto with calamari

This is a very simple yet impressive dish, perfect for a date night or a dish to share with friends at a dinner party. It pairs beautifully with a sparkling rosé wine. The squid ink tastes like the sea with a hint of umami and the addition of fresh lemon juice and clean parsley is perfect.

Bring the fish stock to the boil in a saucepan over a medium heat, then reduce heat to low and keep it hot.

Meanwhile, heat olive oil in a large heavy-based saucepan over a low heat. Add the onion and garlic and sauté until the onion is soft and translucent. Increase the heat, add the calamari and cook fo 3–4 minutes, until opaque and crispy around the edges. Season to taste with salt and freshly ground black pepper.

Add the rice, squid ink and rosé wine and cook over a medium heat until absorbed, then add 250 ml/1 cup of hot stock at a time and cook, stirring until stock is absorbed, then continue adding more stock, 250 ml/1 cup at a time, until the stock is absorbed. Cook until the rice is al dente, adding more water if the risotto is too dry. Add the spinach and lemon juice, to taste, and fold in till the leaves just wilt.

Season to taste and serve immediately with chopped fresh parsley scattered over to top.

750 ml/3 cups fish stock

2 tablespoons olive oil

1 onion, finely chopped

2 garlic cloves, crushed

500 g/1 lb. 2 oz. calamari, cleaned and cut

100 g/3½ oz. thinly shredded spinach leaves

350 g/scant 2 cups risotto rice

2 teaspoons squid ink

250 ml/1 cup dry rosé wine

100 g/4 oz. fresh spinach leaves

freshly squeezed juice of 1 lemon

30 g/1 oz. flat-leaf parsley, leaves picked

sea salt and freshly ground black pepper

SERVES 4

Oat-crusted fish fingers with smashed pea mayo

The super-crispy herby crust on the fish works well with the smashed pea mayo – this is somewhere between a tartare sauce and fresh smashed peas, and is just the best combo. This could easily be turned into a fish-and-chips meal with the addition of French fries, or serve as part of a sharing table.

Season the fish strips with salt and freshly ground black pepper. Pour the beaten eggs into a bowl, tip the flour into a second bowl and sprinkle the oatmeal, quinoa flakes, parsley and chives onto a plate. Dip each fish slice in the flour, then in the egg and finally into the oatmeal mixture, ensuring the fish strips are coated on all sides.

Pour enough oil into a large frying pan/skillet to just cover the base of the pan. Heat the oil over a medium to high heat. When the oil is hot, add the prepared fish strips, in batches, and fry for 6–8 minutes, turning once, or until crisp and golden-brown and completely cooked through. Remove from the pan using a slotted spoon and set aside to drain on paper towels, keeping warm. Repeat the process with the remaining fish.

Meanwhile in a separate bowl, mix all the pea mayo ingredients together and check for seasoning. Serve alongside the fish fingers/fish sticks with a few lemon wedges for squeezing and garnished with sea fennel (or fennel fronds) if using.

800 g/1¾ lb. haddock fillets, cut into strips

2 eggs, beaten

100 g/¾ cup plain/all-purpose flour (gluten-free)

150 g/generous 1 cup oatmeal

50 g/½ cup quinoa flakes

1 tablespoon finely chopped parsley

1 tablespoon finely chopped chives

sea salt and freshly ground black pepper

sunflower oil, for frying

lemon wedges, to serve

sea fennel (or fennel fronds), to garnish (optional)

SMASHED PEA MAYO

300 g/1⅓ cups mayonnaise

200 g/1⅓ cups fresh or frozen peas (thawed if frozen), crushed

2 tablespoons chopped gherkins

2 tablespoons capers, chopped

finely grated zest and freshly squeezed juice of 1 lime

a dash of Tabasco

SERVES 4

Stuffed vine leaves with garlic-herb dressing

These dolmades are made throughout the Balkans and Middle East. There are many variations, but I prefer them with a very simple filling and drizzled with zingy garlic dressing. The filling here is a mixture of rice and quinoa and a lot of herbs as they make for a lighter dish, and one suitable for vegans, vegetarians and flexitarians alike.

Heat the olive oil in a sauté pan, add the spring onions/scallions, onion and garlic and sauté for 10–15 minutes, until softened and caramelized. Add the rice and cook for 2 minutes. Add the stock and stir. Lower the heat and simmer for about 5 minutes, until the rice soaks up the liquid.

When ready, remove the pan from the heat, stir in the cooked quinoa and set aside to rest for at least 10 minutes. Add the coriander/cilantro, dill, mint, lime zest and juice, mix to combine and season with salt and pepper.

Spread 4–5 vine leaves, lemon slices and lemon juice on the base of a 22-cm/9-inch casserole dish. Lay a vine leaf flat with veins facing up and shiny side down. Add 1 tablespoon of filling in the centre, fold the sides of the vine leaf inwards, then roll up the vine leaf to enclose the filling. Transfer to the dish, placing the stuffed vine leaves in a row, one next to the other. Repeat the process, add to the layers until all the filling is used.

Drizzle over some olive oil and cover the stuffed vine leaves with a plate (so that they don't fall apart while cooking). Add enough warm or hot water to completely cover them. Simmer for 40–50 minutes until the rice is done and the vine leaves are tender.

For the dressing, in a food processor add the garlic, mustard, lemon zest and juice and sugar and with the machine on the lowest setting drizzle in all the olive oil until it's emulsified, then stir in the herbs.

When the vine leaves are ready, remove from heat and set them aside to cool in the pot. Serve drizzled with the garlic-herb dressing.

4 tablespoons olive oil, plus extra to drizzle

1 bunch spring onions/scallions, finely chopped

1 onion, finely chopped

2 garlic cloves, crushed

250 g/generous 1¼ cups short-grain rice

200 ml/scant 1 cup vegetable stock

100 g/½ cup cooked mixed tricolore quinoa grains

½ bunch coriander/cilantro, finely chopped

½ bunch dill, finely chopped

½ bunch mint, leaves picked and chopped

finely grated zest and freshly squeezed juice of 1 lime

freshly squeezed juice and finely grated zest of 1 lemon, plus 1 lemon, sliced

250 g/9 oz. vine leaves, from a jar

sea salt and freshly ground black pepper

GARLIC-HERB DRESSING

3 garlic cloves, crushed

1 teaspoon Dijon/French mustard

finely grated zest and freshly squeezed juice of 1 lemon

a pinch of sugar

60 ml/¼ cup olive oil

a handful each of flat-leaf parsley, dill and mint, finely chopped

SERVES 4

Fried polenta
& olive fritters

Little salty, savoury textured taste explosions – the perfect accompaniment to a glass of beer and great for a games night or Sunday drinks and nibbles.

Heat the milk in a saucepan over a medium heat to just about boiling point, then add the polenta/cornmeal and cook according to the pack instructions – usually about 6–8 minutes. Season generously with salt and pepper, then add half the cheese, the green olives, spring onions/scallions, parsley, lemon zest, egg and the tablespoon of cornflour/cornstarch and mix together well.

Cover the polenta with parchment paper to stop a crust forming and set aside until cool enough to handle.

Stir in the remaining cheese, then roll the polenta mixture into 2.5-cm/1-inch balls (you should get about 20 balls). Place on a plate and chill in the fridge for about 1 hour to firm up.

Place the remaining cornflour/cornstarch on a plate and roll the fritters in it, ensuring they are coated on all sides.

Heat the oil into a small pan to 170°C (340°F) – if you don't have a digital thermometer, test if the oil is hot enough by dropping a cube of bread into it; if it sizzles immediately, it's ready.

Carefully fry the fritters, in batches, for about 4 minutes until golden. Remove with a slotted spoon onto paper towels to drain. Keep warm while you cook the remaining balls. Season with salt and serve hot, with lemon wedges for squeezing over.

400 ml/1¾ cups full-fat/whole milk or a plant-based alternative

150 g/1 cup quick-cook polenta/cornmeal

150 g/2¼ cups finely grated Parmesan (or vegetarian alternative)

200 g/2 cups pitted green olives, chopped

1 bunch spring onions/scallions, finely chopped

15 g/½ oz. parsley, finely chopped (a good handful)

finely grated zest of 1 lemon, plus wedges to serve

1 egg, beaten

1 tablespoon cornflour/cornstarch, plus 70 g/scant ¾ cup for coating

sea salt and freshly ground black pepper

vegetable oil, for deep-frying

SERVES 6–8

Pecorino arancini with roasted cherry tomato sauce

Classic, moreish, crowd-pleasing and just simply delicious. This is the perfect way to use up leftover risotto, or just make them from scratch. You can stuff the arancini with an array of fillings, from mozzarella to goat's cheese or chopped ham. This recipe uses pecorino – a hard sheep's milk cheese, with a tangy flavour – while the addition of ricotta adds a creaminess.

Heat the oil in a saucepan over low heat, add onion and stir occasionally until tender. Add the crushed garlic and the rice, stir to coat, then add the stock, little by little, until rice is slightly overcooked and stock is absorbed. Add the thyme, grated pecorino, ricotta and nutmeg and stir until creamy. Remove from heat and spread the mixture out in a tray. Cool to room temperature, then refrigerate for 1–1½ hours.

Meanwhile, make the sauce. Preheat the oven to 180°C (350°F) Gas 4. In a baking dish add the tomatoes on the vine with the garlic cloves, 2 tablespoons of the olive oil, honey, dried chilli flakes/hot red pepper flakes and salt and pepper. Roast in the preheated oven for 25 minutes, then add a few tablespoons of water, remove the vine and crush the tomatoes. Set aside.

Shape walnut-sized balls of the chilled rice mixture with your hands, then push a pecorino cube into centre of each, pressing rice around to enclose completely. Roll the rice balls in flour, then in beaten egg and finally in breadcrumbs, shaking off excess in between, ensuring they are completely coated. Place on a tray and chill in the fridge for 30 minutes.

Preheat the oil in a deep saucepan or deep-fryer to 200°C (400°F). Deep-fry arancini in batches for 2–3 minutes, until golden brown and crispy, turning occasionally. Place the roasted cherry tomato sauce on serving plates, drizzle over the remaining olive oil and serve with the hot arancini to top, scattered with thyme.

50 ml/3½ tablespoons olive oil

1 onion, finely chopped

2 garlic cloves, crushed

200 g/generous 1 cup Arborio risotto rice

750 ml/3 cups vegetable stock

5 sprigs lemon thyme, leaves picked

150 g/5½ oz. pecorino (⅔ grated and ⅓ cut into 20 cubes)

100 g/scant ½ cup ricotta

½ teaspoon ground nutmeg

plain/all-purpose flour, for coating

2 eggs, lightly beaten

250 g/4½ cups fine soft white breadcrumbs

sunflower oil, for deep-frying

ROASTED CHERRY TOMATO SAUCE

500 g/1 lb. 2 oz. cherry tomatoes on the vine

4 garlic cloves, smashed

3 tablespoons olive oil

2 tablespoons honey

a pinch of dried chilli flakes/ hot red pepper flakes

sea salt and freshly ground black pepper

20 g/⅔ oz. fresh lemon thyme, leaves picked, to garnish

SERVES 4–6

Rice pancakes with spiced potatoes

Similar to Southern India's dosas, this pancake base uses rice and urad dal that are first soaked for a few hours, and then left overnight. As it soaks, it gently ferments which adds a delicate flavour and a little bubble to the mixture. Served alongside spiced potatoes, you'll be transported to busy markets and the street-food vendors of India.

Place the rice flour in a bowl, add just enough cold water to cover and leave to soak for 2–3 hours.

Rinse the urad dal, place in a bowl with enough cold water to cover them and soak for 2–3 hours. Drain the lentils, then place in an electric blender and grind, adding just enough water to form a thick fine paste.

Mix the ground lentil paste with the soaked rice flour until you get a thick batter. Add salt to taste and leave the batter in a warm place overnight to ferment.

The next morning, make the spiced potatoes. Cook the potatoes in a saucepan of simmering salted water for 25–30 minutes until tender, then drain well and set aside. Heat the oil in a large frying pan/skillet, add the onion, ginger, garlic and curry leaves and cook for 7–8 minutes until the onion is soft, then add spices and stir until fragrant. Add potatoes and 80 ml/⅓ cup water, cover and simmer for 3–5 minutes for the flavours to combine and potatoes are very soft. Stir in the coriander/cilantro, mint and green chilli/chile and season to taste.

Mix the batter thoroughly again – it should be a thin pancake consistency (add water if it's too thick). Add a little ghee to a frying pan/skillet until it is hot. Pour a ladleful of the batter into the centre and spread evenly in circles until it reaches the edges of the pan. Fry for 2–3 minutes per side, turning once, until golden and crisp. Wipe out the pan with paper towels and repeat with remaining ghee and batter. Top the pancakes with the spiced potatoes, coconut, green chilli/chile and chilli/chili powder and serve with tamarind chutney and lime wedges for squeezing.

300 g/2¼ cups rice flour

100 g/generous ½ cup part urad dal (split black lentils)

1 teaspoon fenugreek seeds

50 g/2 oz. ghee

sea salt

SPICED POTATOES

800 g/1¾ lb. potatoes, peeled and cut into 3-cm/1¼-inch pieces

60 ml/¼ cup vegetable oil

1 onion, finely chopped

a thumb-sized piece of fresh ginger, grated

2 garlic cloves, finely chopped

5 fresh curry leaves

1 teaspoon mustard seeds

1 teaspoon ground coriander

1 teaspoon ground turmeric

30 g/1 oz. mixed coriander/ cilantro and mint, leaves picked

1 long green chilli/chile, finely chopped

sea salt and freshly ground black pepper

TO SERVE

grated coconut

sliced green chilli/chile

chilli/chili powder

tamarind chutney

lime wedges, for squeezing

SERVES 4–6

Seedy rye & oat crispbread with pickled cucumber tzatziki & piyaz

These crispbreads are simplicity itself to make and super tasty. You can enjoy them as an anytime snack with a variety of toppings, or use them as dippers. Here I've served them with a tangy pickled yogurt and cucumber tzatziki dip, along with a Turkish-style piyaz – a simple white bean salad with red onion and tomatoes. Add other small plates to make a mezze to share.

Preheat the oven to 160°C (340°F) Gas 3. Take out two large baking sheets and a roll of parchment paper.

For the crispbread, add the dried ingredients to a very large bowl, stir with your hands, then tip in the oil and water. Stir very well to mix together.

Take three sheets of parchment paper and place the baking sheets on them and pull up on all sides of the paper to form the shape of the trays. This will be your rolling guide. Halve the dough and place on one piece of paper, then lay another piece of paper on top. Roll as thinly as you can, patching and shaping as you go. Peel off the top paper and lay the dough with the underneath paper on one of the baking sheets. Lightly score into pieces with a sharp knife, if you wish. Repeat with the remaining dough.

Place the trays in the preheated oven and bake for 15 minutes. Swap the baking sheets around and bake for a further 15 minutes. Do another swap and bake for 10–15 minutes until quite golden. Let cool and break into pieces, or crack along the scored lines with a heavy knife. Store in an airtight container for up to 2 weeks.

For the pickled cucumber tzatziki, mix all the ingredients together, season well and set aside.

For the piyaz, combine the onion and sumac in a bowl and mix well, then add the tomatoes, beans, parsley, olive oil and lemon juice. Season well.

50 g/½ cup rolled/old-fashioned oats

150 g/1 cup rye flour

50 g/6 tablespoons each ground flaxseeds/linseeds, sesame seeds, sunflower seeds and pumpkin seeds

1 teaspoon fennel seeds cracked

1 teaspoon black sesame seeds

1 teaspoon cumin seeds

¼ teaspoon dried chilli flakes/hot red pepper flakes

1 teaspoon sea salt flakes

80 ml/⅓ cup extra virgin olive oil

60 ml/¼ cup warm water

PICKLED CUCUMBER TZATZIKI

150 g/5½ oz. cucumber, grated

finely grated zest and freshly squeezed juice of ½ a lemon

500 g/2¼ cups Greek yogurt

2 tablespoons olive oil

1 garlic clove, crushed

70 g/2½ oz. pickled gherkins, julienned, plus 2 teaspoons gherkin water

sea salt and freshly ground black pepper

PIYAZ

1 red onion, thinly sliced

1 teaspoon ground sumac

300 g/10½ oz. cherry tomatoes, deseeded and diced

400-g/14-oz. can cannellini beans, drained

10g/½ cup finely shredded flat-leaf parsley

60 ml/¼ cup olive oil

freshly squeezed juice of 1 lemon

sea salt and freshly ground black pepper

SERVES 4

Bowls

Avocado & kale grain bowl with tahini-coriander dressing

These bowls can be prepared ahead for either a light lunch at home or for work meals for the week. Pouches of ready-cooked mixed grains, with extra flavours added, can be bought from most supermarkets.

Combine the kale, olive oil and lemon juice and zest in a bowl, season and massage kale with your fingers until it wilts. Add the spring onions/scallions, chickpeas and mixed grains, and toss to combine.

For the dressing, whisk the ingredients together in a bowl, then thin with 2–3 tablespoons of hot water to drizzling consistency and season to taste.

Divide the kale mixture between 2 serving bowls and scatter with the feta. Dip one half of the cut-side of the avocado in dukkah, place on top of the kale mixture and arrange the courgette/zucchini and olives next to it. Drizzle with the dressing to taste and serve scattered with pistachio nuts.

1 bunch kale, stems discarded, torn into bite-sized pieces

3 tablespoons extra-virgin olive oil

finely grated zest and freshly squeezed juice of 2 lemons

4 spring onions/scallions, finely chopped

400 g/14 oz. mixed cooked grains

400-g/14-oz. can chickpeas, drained

120 g/4 oz. feta, crumbled (or vegan equivalent)

1 avocado, halved, stoned/pitted and peeled

2 tablespoons dukkah, plus extra to finish

1 courgette/zucchini, grated

50 g/½ cup pitted green olives

pistachio nuts, coarsely chopped, to serve

TAHINI-CORIANDER/CILANTRO DRESSING

30 g/1 oz. coriander/cilantro, leaves and stalks

1 teaspoon ground coriander

1 teaspoon ground cumin

70 ml/scant ⅓ cup extra-virgin olive oil

60 ml/¼ cup tahini

1 garlic clove, crushed

freshly squeezed juice of 1 lemon

sea salt and freshly ground black pepper

SERVES 2

Dashi rice green tea broth bowl

A light, clean and refreshing bowl of goodness, this is the loveliest combination of prawns/shrimp, sugar snap peas and tofu – so nourishing for the mind and body. However, it can easily become a vegetable-based dashi broth by adding extra greens and omitting the prawns/shrimp.

Whisk the dashi and boiling water in a large saucepan over a high heat, add the rice and soy sauce and bring to the boil. Reduce the heat to medium-high and cook for 15–20 minutes until the rice is just tender. Add the green tea bags, prawns/shrimp, greens, sugar snap peas and ginger, remove the pan from the heat, and stir in the cubed tofu just to gently heat. Let stand for 3–4 minutes until the prawns/shrimp are cooked through and the greens wilted.

Ladle the soup into warm bowls, discarding the green tea bags. Scatter with watercress sprigs, and serve hot.

2 sachets instant dashi

2 litres/quarts boiling water

220 g/scant 1¼ cups sushi rice, rinsed under cold running water

60 ml/¼ cup soy sauce, plus extra to taste

2–3 green tea bags

16 medium uncooked prawns/shrimp, peeled

200 g/7 oz. mixed Asian greens

20 g/¾ oz. sugar snap peas, trimmed

a thumb-sized piece of fresh ginger, grated

200 g/7 oz. tofu, cut into cubes

a little watercress, to garnish

SERVES 4

Bibimbap-y bowl

The most well-known of Korean dishes, this humble rice bowl is topped with all sorts of seasoned sautéed vegetables, marinated meat (usually beef), traditionally served with a fried egg sunny-side up and finished with a sprinkle of sesame and generous dollop of a sweet-spicy-savoury gochujang sauce. My take is a lighter vegetarian version with 7-minute boiled eggs, rather than fried, but super tasty nonetheless. You can have a play with the toppings as you like.

For the pickled carrots, stir the vinegar, sugar, salt and 250 ml/1 cup hot water together in a saucepan over a medium heat to dissolve sugar. Set aside to cool, then add the carrot and stand for 1 hour to pickle. Drain the carrot from pickling liquid before serving.

Cook the rice for 12 minutes in a pan of boiling water, drain, then remove from the heat and stand, covered, for 5 minutes.

For the shiitake, heat a frying pan/skillet to a medium heat, add the sesame oil, then the mushrooms and sauté for a few minutes. In a bowl mix the other ingredients and pour into the mushrooms. Cook for another minute, then remove from the heat and set aside.

For the spinach, blanch the spinach leaves until just wilted, refresh in iced water, drain and squeeze dry.

For gochujang sauce, combine the ingredients in a bowl and set aside.

Sauté the mooli/daikon and garlic in sesame oil in a frying pan/skillet over a low heat until just tender. Season to taste and set aside.

Season the cucumber ribbons with chilli/chili powder and salt and set aside.

To serve, divide the rice among individual serving bowls, add the kimchi, pickled carrots, shiitake and spinach on top. Top each with a boiled egg half and serve hot with the gochujang sauce drizzled over.

400 g/2 cups short-grain brown rice, rinsed
250 g/9 oz. mooli/daikon, julienned on a mandoline
1 garlic clove, crushed
1 tablespoon sesame oil
1 cucumber, shaved into ribbons
2 teaspoons smoked chilli/chili powder
2 eggs, boiled for 7 minutes
2 teaspoons vegetable oil
80 g/3 oz. kimchi, chopped
salt

PICKLED CARROTS
60 ml/¼ cup rice wine vinegar
55 g/¼ cup caster/granulated sugar
2 teaspoons salt
1 large carrot, julienned on a mandoline

FRIED SHIITAKE
1 tablespoon sesame oil
200 g/7 oz. shiitake mushrooms
2 tablespoons tamari or soy sauce
2 tablespoons sake
1 tablespoon rice vinegar
1½ teaspoons brown sugar

WILTED SPINACH
200 g/7 oz. fresh spinach

GOCHUJANG SAUCE
2 tablespoons gochujang
1 tablespoon rice wine vinegar
1 tablespoon soy sauce
1 teaspoon sesame oil
2 teaspoons roasted sesame seeds
2 teaspoons Korean rice malt syrup

SERVES 4

Dirty fried rice

A fusion of naughty and nice, perfect for a late night snack or a lazy Sunday. The dressed spinach is to add fresh greens, but the rice is also delicious on its own. It all depends how naughty you are feeling!

Start by cooking the rice in a saucepan filled with water and the chicken stock cubes, according to the package instructions (for wholegrain basmati usually 25 minutes), drain well and set aside.

Heat the rapeseed/canola oil in a large frying pan/skillet or wok and heat to medium-high. Add the bacon and cook until medium brown and crispy around the edges, then add the onion with a pinch of salt and turn the heat down to medium. Cook, stirring, for a good 10 minutes, allowing the onion to caramelize.

Add the celery, ginger, garlic, soy sauce, fish sauce, maple syrup, tomato purée/paste and paprika or chilli/chili powder and cook for a further 6–8 minutes, but don't allow the pan to dry out. At this point add a couple of tablespoons water and scrape the base of the pan to release all the crispy bits. Add the coriander/cilantro stems and rice. Stir and mix all the flavours and cook for 2–3 minutes.

Meanwhile, place the spinach in a bowl and add the lime juice, a pinch of salt and pepper and the olive oil. Toss together.

Serve the rice in bowls with the dressed spinach, reserved coriander/cilantro, reserved celery leaves, spring onions/scallions and jalapeños for extra kick.

250 g/generous 1⅓ cups wholegrain basmati rice

2 chicken stock cubes

2 tablespoons rapeseed/canola oil

180 g/6½ oz. streaky/fatty bacon, finely chopped

1 onion, finely diced

4 celery stalks, finely diced (reserve the leaves)

a thumb-sized piece of fresh ginger, grated

3 garlic cloves, crushed

2 tablespoons soy sauce

1 tablespoon fish sauce

1 tablespoon maple syrup

1 tablespoon tomato purée/paste

1 teaspoon hot smoked paprika or chilli/chili powder

½ bunch coriander/cilantro, stems finely chopped (top leaves and stalks reserved to finish)

sea salt

TO FINISH

80 g/3 oz. baby spinach

freshly squeezed juice of 2 limes

olive oil, to dress

4 spring onions/scallions, thinly sliced

1 tablespoon chopped jalapeños (optional)

sea salt and freshly ground black pepper

SERVES 4

Black & white bowl

A bed of black rice topped with white fish and mushrooms, this is a simple and elegant dish, gently flavoured with a Japanese-inspired miso-ginger dressing.

Place the rinsed rice, salt and 1 litre/quart water in a saucepan and set aside to soak for 1 hour. Bring the pan to a simmer, then reduce the heat to low, cover with a tight-fitting lid and cook without uncovering for 25 minutes. Remove the pan from the heat and stand covered for 10 minutes, then stir in soy sauce, mirin, rice vinegar and sesame seeds.

For the white miso dressing, whisk the miso, vinegar and lemon juice in a bowl to combine, then whisk in the oils, ginger and garlic. Thin with a little water if necessary to achieve a drizzling consistency.

Meanwhile, heat a frying pan/skillet to medium heat, add 1 tablespoon of the sesame oil and sauté the chestnut/cremini mushrooms for a few minutes (just to soften), then add the enoki for another few minutes and set aside. Wipe the pan out ready for the cod.

Brush the cod with the white miso and remaining tablespoon of sesame oil. Heat the pan to a medium heat, then add the cod and cook, without moving it at all, for about 2–3 minutes or until the skin is golden and crisp. If you are cooking without the skin, the fish should also be golden. Carefully turn the cod over to cook the other side – the fish is ready when it has lost its opaque texture.

Divide the warm rice between serving bowls, top with the cod and cooking juices, cabbage and mushrooms. Drizzle generously with the white miso dressing, scatter with extra sesame seeds, spring onions/scallions and iceplant leaves or samphire (if using) and serve.

- 400 g/generous 2 cups black rice, rinsed
- 1 teaspoon sea salt
- 2 tablespoons soy sauce
- 2 teaspoons mirin
- 2 teaspoons rice vinegar
- 1 tablespoon mixed black and white sesame seeds, plus extra to serve
- 2 tablespoons sesame oil
- 200 g/7 oz. chestnut/cremini mushrooms
- 60 g/2 oz. enoki mushrooms, trimmed
- 2 x cod fillets, skin on (approx 200 g/7 oz. each)
- 2 tablespoons white miso
- 150 g/5½ oz. white cabbage, very thinly shaved on a mandoline
- spring onions/scallions, thinly sliced, to serve
- edible iceplant leaves or samphire, to garnish (optional)

WHITE MISO DRESSING
- 1 tablespoon shiro miso
- 1 tablespoon rice vinegar
- 1 tablespoon freshly squeezed lemon juice
- 2 tablespoons vegetable oil
- 2 teaspoons sesame oil
- 1 teaspoon finely grated ginger
- ½ garlic clove, finely grated

SERVES 2

Brown shrimp
nasi goreng-style rice

Nasi goreng refers to fried rice in both Indonesian and Malay. Here I've added a little twist by frying brown shrimp with the rice for extra protein. The dish is simply served with chopped tomatoes, cucumber, some peanuts and crispy shallots for crunchy, fresh textures.

Put the rice in a saucepan with the boiling water. Stir once, bring to a simmer, then cover and turn the heat right down. Cook for 15 minutes, then take off the heat and cover with a damp tea towel or cloth for 5 minutes with the lid off. Fork through to fluff up.

Meanwhile put all the ingredients for the paste in a small blender or mortar and whizz or pound until fairly smooth.

Heat the 2 tablespoons of oil in a wok over a high heat, then fry the garlic until golden, add the brown shrimp and cook for a few minutes, then add the spice paste and cook for a minute or so. Add the cooked rice by hand, breaking up any clumps as you go, and fry until heated through, then stir in the kecap manis, soy sauce, spring onions/scallions and chilli/chile.

In a separate frying pan/skillet, heat the butter until it melts. Crack an egg onto a small plate or saucer. Slide it off the saucer into the pan, and repeat with the other one. Cover with a lid and leave for 3 minutes over a low heat. Check the white is set and, if not, leave it for another 30 seconds and then check again. Season. Place the rice mixture on serving plates, top each one with an egg and serve topped with the cucumber, tomatoes, crispy shallots and peanuts.

Add the rice by hand, breaking up any clumps as you go, and fry until heated through, then stir in the kecap manis, soy sauce, spring onions/scallions and chilli/chile. Serve with cucumber, tomatoes, crispy shallots and peanuts.

200 g/scant 1 cup jasmine rice

400 ml/1¾ cups boiling water

2 tablespoons peanut/groundnut oil

2 garlic cloves, crushed

200 g/7 oz. brown shrimp

2 tablespoons kecap manis

2 teaspoons soy sauce

4 spring onions/scallions

1 green chilli/chile, halved lengthways

a knob/pat of butter

2 eggs

PASTE

50 g/2 oz. shallots, roughly chopped

1 garlic clove, roughly chopped

2 teaspoons Indonesian shrimp paste

1 red chilli/chile, deseeded

1 tablespoon peanut/groundnut oil

TO SERVE

1 cucumber, roughly chopped

2–3 tomatoes, roughly chopped

2 tablespoons crispy shallots

2 tablespoons peanuts, toasted

SERVES 2

Vietnamese-style rice bowl with chicken skewers & nuoc cham

This Vietnamese-inspired rice bowl encompasses the five flavours and elements of Vietnamese cuisine: sweet, sour, bitter, spicy and salty. The charred chicken skewers on the bed of rice, the fresh salad, the herbs and the citrus, spicy sweet and sour sauce all come together for a taste sensation.

For the chicken skewers, whisk together everything except the chicken together in a small bowl for 1 minute until combined and the sugar is starting to dissolve. Add the chicken chunks and stir to coat. Refrigerate overnight or for at least 4 hours. Meanwhile, soak 8 long wooden skewers in water for at least an hour. Fire up the grill/broiler and allow it to become hot and fiery. Add a few chunks of chicken to each skewer and grill/broil until the chicken is cooked through and there's a nice char on the nuggets. Remove from the heat and set aside.

To make the nuoc cham, add 3 tablespoons of water and the palm sugar/jaggery to a bowl and stir for 1 minute until dissolved. Add in the lime juice, fish sauce, garlic and chillies/chiles.

To cook the rice, heat the rapeseed/canola oil in a saucepan, add the onion and soften for a few minutes, then add the rice and turmeric and cook for a further minute. Add the ginger, lemongrass and 500 ml/2 cups of water, bring to simmer and cook, covered, for 15 minutes. Turn off the heat. In a separate bowl dissolve the palm sugar/jaggery in the fish sauce and lime juice and pour into the rice, fluffing it up with a fork. Keep covered until ready to serve.

To serve, divide the rice between bowls, top with the chicken skewers and add the mint, coriander/cilantro, carrot, cucumber, lettuce, peanuts, lime wedges, nuoc cham and some sriracha for some extra kick.

CHICKEN SKEWERS

½ onion, finely chopped

3 garlic cloves, crushed

30 g/1 oz. palm sugar/jaggery

2 tablespoons soy sauce

1 tablespoon fish sauce

2 tablespoons sesame oil

500 g/1 lb. 2 oz. chicken breast, cut into chunks

NUOC CHAM

2 tablespoons palm sugar/jaggery

freshly squeezed juice of 1 lime

2 tablespoons fish sauce

1 garlic clove, crushed

1–2 bird's eye chillies/bird chiles, chopped

RICE

1 tablespoon rapeseed/canola oil

½ onion, finely chopped

250 g/1⅓ cups jasmine rice

½ teaspoon ground turmeric

a thumb-sized piece of fresh ginger, grated

1 lemongrass stalk, bruised

1 tablespoon palm sugar/jaggery

2 tablespoons fish sauce

freshly squeezed juice of 1 lime

TO SERVE

30 g/1 oz. mint, leaves picked

30 g/1 oz. coriander/cilantro, leaves picked

1 carrot, julienned

1 cucumber, julienned

2 Little Gem/Bibb lettuces, leaves separated

2 tablespoons peanuts, toasted

2 limes, cut into wedges

sriracha

SERVES 4

Curry-spiced pearl barley soup

This is the perfect dish for a healthy curry night. If you want to add extra goodness, swirl through some wilted spinach or just a dollop of yogurt. It's surprisingly simple to make, and the pearl barley adds a creaminess. Finishing the soup with tempered spices adds another layer of flavour.

Rinse the split peas well, drain and set aside.

Heat the coconut oil in a saucepan over a medium-high heat. Add the onion and sauté until just tender and starting to turn golden, then stir through the garlic, cinnamon, curry powder and smoked paprika until fragrant. Add the split peas to the pan along with the coconut milk and vegetable stock. Bring to the boil, lower the heat to medium and simmer, stirring occasionally, until the spilt peas are tender and start to fall apart – this should take about 1 hour. Then add the pearl barley and cook for a further 30 minutes, until the barley is tender.

For the tempered spices, heat the coconut oil in a saucepan over a high heat. Add the seeds and stir until fragrant, then add the curry leaves and remove from the heat.

Serve the soup with tempered spices spooned over, topped with a dollop of yogurt (if using) and warmed naan breads on the side.

250 g/1¼ cups split peas
1 tablespoon coconut oil
1 onion, finely chopped
2 garlic cloves, crushed
1 cinnamon stick
2 tablespoons curry powder
1 tablespoon smoked paprika
400 ml/1¾ cups coconut milk
1 litre/quart vegetable stock
150 g/¾ cup pearl barley

TEMPERED SPICES
1 tablespoon coconut oil
½ teaspoon fenugreek seeds
1 teaspoon yellow mustard seeds
a handful of fresh curry leaves

TO SERVE
naan breads
about 4 tablespoons plain/ natural yogurt (optional)

SERVES 4

Chirashi-zushi

This tuna dish is just like sushi but in a bowl. The addition of plums adds an element of surprise and brown rice brings an extra nuttiness, but otherwise the same but different!

Cook the rice in a saucepan of boiling salted water according to the package instructions until tender, then drain well and transfer to a bowl. Add the rice vinegar, maple syrup and ginger and stir the rice gently until thoroughly mixed. Set the rice aside for 15–20 minutes, stirring occasionally, until cool.

Meanwhile, for the sesame tuna, place a large non-stick frying pan/skillet over a medium-high heat. Rub the miso all over the tuna, then pat on the sesame seeds to cover. Place in the hot pan with 1 tablespoon of olive oil and sear for 1½ minutes on each side, so it is beautifully golden on the outside but blushing in the middle. Remove the tuna from the pan and slice, ready to serve.

Divide the rice between 2 serving bowls, top with the seared tuna, radish, plum wedges, spring onions/scallions, avocado with lime juice, roe, sesame oil to taste, sesame seeds, toasted nori, shiso and pickled ginger. Serve with wasabi and soy sauce on the side.

400 g/2 cups short-grain brown rice, rinsed

80 ml/⅓ cup rice vinegar

1 teaspoon maple syrup

a thumb-sized piece of fresh ginger, grated

400 g/14 oz. tuna (sushi grade)

1 tablespoon miso

3 tablespoons black sesame seeds

1 tablespoon olive oil

TO SERVE

4 radishes, julienned

1 plum, cut into thin wedges

4 spring onions/scallions, thinly sliced

1 avocado, thinly sliced

freshly squeezed juice of 1 lime

50 g/2 oz. salmon roe

a few drops of sesame oil

1 tablespoon toasted sesame seeds

toasted nori

shiso leaves

pickled ginger

wasabi

soy sauce

SERVES 2

Chilli crab & coconut rice

Singapore is famous for its chilli crab and it is always such a treat to make this at home. The crab needs to be very fresh when cooked and this does require some effort, but it is so worth it! Alternatively, you can substitute the crab for 1 kg/2 lb. 2 oz. of unshelled tiger prawn/jumbo shrimp. The fun is in the mess that this makes – serve the seafood in its shell and everyone can dig in. The coconut rice is the perfect vehicle for all the juices.

Whisk cornflour/cornstarch and 200 ml/scant 1 cup water in a small bowl to combine and set aside.

Process the chillies/chiles and onion in a food processor until a paste forms and set aside.

Heat the vegetable oil in a large wok over a medium heat. Add the crab and stir-fry until it starts to colour. Remove the crab using a slotted spoon and set aside. You'll be using the wok again.

Meanwhile, for the coconut rice, place all the ingredients except the rice in a saucepan and bring to a simmer over a medium-high heat. Add the rice and stir until it returns to the simmer. Cover, reduce the heat to very low and cook for 15–20 minutes until the rice is tender. Remove from the heat and allow to stand for 5 minutes.

Add the chilli/chile paste to the wok over a medium–high heat and stir until tender. Add the ginger and garlic and stir until fragrant . Add the tomato purée/paste and stir until the mixture darkens in colour. Add the fresh tomatoes and sriracha and 100 ml/scant ½ cup water. Bring to a simmer, then add the cornflour/cornstarch mixture and stir to combine, then add crab and cook, stirring occasionally, until orange and cooked through. Drizzle with egg, stir to coat, season to taste with soy sauce, fish sauce, sugar and salt. Serve hot, topped with coriander/cilantro, spring onions/scallions, lime wedges and coconut rice.

½ teaspoon cornflour/cornstarch

3 red long chillies/chiles

1 onion, finely chopped

80 ml/⅓ cup vegetable oil

2 crabs (jointed by your fishmonger)

a thumb-sized piece of fresh ginger, grated

3 garlic cloves, crushed

1 tablespoon tomato purée/paste

6 tomatoes, roughly chopped

1 tablespoon sriracha

1 egg, lightly beaten

2 tablespoons light soy sauce

1 tablespoon fish sauce

1–2 tablespoons palm sugar/jaggery

salt

COCONUT RICE

400 ml/1¾ cups coconut milk

200 ml/scant 1 cup fresh young coconut water

1 teaspoon each cumin and coriander seeds, finely ground in a mortar and pestle

1 teaspoon fish paste

2 lemongrass stalks, white part only, finely chopped

1 teaspoon salt

400 g/2¼ cups jasmine rice, rinsed

TO SERVE

coriander/cilantro

thinly sliced spring onions/scallions

lime wedges

SERVES 4–6

Barley & wild rice with candied salted almonds & barberries

Candied salted almonds, tart and sour barberries, grains, sumac and dried rose petals – all evoke images of eastern feasts, mint tea, incense burning and people coming together. This rice dish can be served alongside slow roasts, barbecued meats and vegetables or on its own with crumbled soft goat's cheese.

For the candied salted almonds, preheat the oven to 180°C (350°F) Gas 4 and line a baking sheet with parchment paper. Stir the sugar with 2 tablespoons of water in a saucepan over a low heat until the sugar dissolves. Add the almonds, stir to coat, then tip onto the baking sheet and bake in the preheated oven for about 10 minutes, stirring occasionally, until lightly caramelized. Set aside.

Meanwhile, place the barley in a saucepan of cold salted water. Then place 200 g/generous 1 cup of the wild rice in a second pan of cold salted water. Bring both pans to the boil over medium-high heat, then reduce to medium and simmer for 20–25 minutes, until tender but not falling apart. Drain and set aside.

To make the dressing, in a bowl mix the olive oil, lemon juice, sumac, salt and sliced onion and let it sit for at least 20 minutes.

Heat the vegetable oil in a saucepan to 200°C (400°F). Add the remaining wild rice and fry until puffed. Remove with a metal sieve/strainer and drain on paper towels.

Toss the barley and wild rice with the barberries and the dressing, then tip into a serving bowl and scatter with rose petals, mint leaves, candied almonds and puffed wild rice. Crumble over the goat's cheese, if using, and serve.

150 g/generous ¾ cup barley

250 g/1⅓ cups wild rice

2 tablespoons dried barberries

salt

vegetable oil, for deep-frying

CANDIED SALTED ALMONDS

2 tablespoons light soft brown sugar

100 g/¾ cup salted Marcona almonds

DRESSING

60 ml/¼ cup olive oil

freshly squeezed juice of 2 lemons

2 tablespoons sumac

1 teaspoon salt

1 red onion, thinly sliced

TO SERVE

2 tablespoons dried rose petals

30 g/1 oz. mint, leaves picked

soft goat's cheese, crumbled (optional)

SERVES 4 AS A SIDE

Larger Plates

Genovese clams with rice

The simplest of dishes from the Italian region of Genoa, this is a soupier version of risotto, with the clean flavours of clams, wine, lemon and garlic. An elegant dish for entertaining, and even more perfect with a handful of samphire added (when in season). Enjoy with a glass of crisp white wine.

Cook the rice in a large saucepan of boiling water for 12–15 minutes until al dente, drain and return to the pan.

Meanwhile, heat the oil in a large saucepan over a medium-high heat, add onion and garlic and cook, stirring occasionally, for 4–5 minutes until tender.

Meanwhile, heat a third saucepan over a high heat, add the drained clams and wine, cover with a lid and cook for 2–3 minutes, shaking the pan occasionally, until the clams open, then remove from heat. Discard any clams that have not opened.

Using a slotted spoon, transfer the clams to the onion mixture, then strain the cooking liquid over the clams. Add the samphire (if using), the parsley, lemon zest and juice, chillies/chiles and season to taste.

Add the clam mixture to the rice last and stir everything well to combine and just soften and meld the samphire into the rice. Serve hot.

350 g/scant 2 cups risotto rice

2 tablespoons olive oil

1 onion, finely chopped

2 garlic cloves, crushed

1 kg/2¼ lb. clams, soaked in cold water for 20 minutes to remove grit, drained

200 ml/scant 1 cup dry white wine

20 g/½ cup coarsely chopped flat-leaf parsley

finely grated zest and freshly squeezed juice of 2 lemons

1–2 green chillies/chiles (depending on how hot you like it)

a handful of samphire (optional)

salt and freshly ground black pepper

SERVES 4

Freekah & herb salad with preserved lemon & black olives

Roasted shallots with a touch of cinnamon serve as a bed for the freekah, crisp cucumber, tomatoes, olives and the intense citrus but yet mellow preserved lemon. For an extra element, crumble over some feta or add pan-fried halloumi.

Preheat the oven to 180°C (350°F) Gas 4.

Spread the shallots on a small baking sheet. Drizzle with the olive oil, sprinkle with cinnamon and oregano and season to taste. Roast in the preheated oven for 40–45 minutes until tender and caramelized.

Meanwhile, bring 400 ml/1¾ cups water and 1 teaspoon salt to the boil in a saucepan over a medium-high heat. Add the freekah, stir, bring back to the boil and cover with a lid. Reduce the heat to low and cook for 25–30 minutes until the freekah is tender and the water evaporates. Drain and transfer to a bowl.

Mix the dressing ingredients in a serving dish, then add the shallots, freekah, cucumber and tomatoes and mix well. Check for seasoning, then add the herbs and scatter over the almonds. Serve with the addition of crumbled feta or pan-fried halloumi, if you wish.

8 shallots, peeled and halved

2 tablespoons olive oil

a pinch of ground cinnamon

a pinch of dried oregano

200 g/7 oz. freekah, rinsed

50 g/generous ⅓ cup almonds, coarsely chopped and toasted

1 large cucumber, cubed

200 g/7 oz. cherry tomatoes, quartered

1 small bunch each dill, coriander/cilantro, mint and parsley, leaves picked

salt and freshly ground black pepper

feta or pan-fried halloumi, to serve (optional)

DRESSING

100 g/1 cup black olives, stoned/pitted and halved

1 preserved lemon, pith and flesh discarded, skin rinsed and finely chopped

1 garlic clove, crushed

60 ml/¼ cup olive oil

a pinch of ground cinnamon (optional)

freshly squeezed juice of 1–2 lemons, to taste

1 teaspoon honey, or to taste

SERVES 4

Sticky rice parcels with chicken curry

It's so much fun to take a plate of these banana leaf parcels to the table. They contain Thai glutinous rice, which is cooked until soft and sticky and infused with aromatics. Serve alongside this deeply flavoursome chicken curry.

Rinse the rice multiple times until the water runs clear, then cook according to the package instructions and set aside. Heat the vegetable oil in a frying pan/skillet and add the mushrooms, season well and sauté until golden and all the liquid has been cooked out. Place the garlic, ginger, chilli/chile, shallots and lemongrass in a food processor and blend to a paste. Add the paste to the mushrooms and cook for 5 minutes over a medium heat.

Meanwhile, make the chicken curry. Process the shallots, garlic, chilli/chile and ginger in a food processor until finely chopped. Heat the oil in a large saucepan over a medium-high heat, add the chilli mixture and cook stirring occasionally, for 2 minutes until fragrant. Add onion and spices, stir for 2 minutes, then add the chicken and stir to coat well. Add the coconut milk, curry leaf sprig, lemongrass, cinnamon, star anise and 100 ml/scant ½ cup water and simmer for about 45 minutes, or until chicken is cooked through and tender. Season to taste with palm sugar/jaggery and sea salt.

While the chicken is cooking, complete the rice parcels. Add the fish sauce, soy sauce, honey and rice vinegar to the rice mixture. Then take a banana leaf (or square of parchment paper), add a sixth of the rice to the centre, top with a sixth of the mushroom mixture and wrap up like a parcel with string. Repeat with the remaining leaves and filling. Steam for 30 minutes. Serve with the chicken curry, or simply on their own and some sriracha.

CHICKEN CURRY

- 4 each golden shallots, coarsely chopped
- 4 garlic cloves, coarsely chopped
- 4 long red chillies/chiles, coarsely chopped
- a thumb-sized piece of fresh ginger, coarsely chopped
- 2 tablespoons vegetable oil
- I onion, thinly sliced
- 6 cardamom pods, bruised
- I teaspoon ground turmeric
- 8 boneless chicken thighs, cut into strips
- 400 ml/1¾ cups coconut milk
- I fresh curry leaf sprig
- I lemongrass stalk, bruised
- I cinnamon stick
- I star anise
- palm sugar/jaggery, to taste
- sea salt

SERVES 4

STICKY RICE PARCELS

- 180 g/I cup glutinous rice
- 2 tablespoons vegetable oil
- 250 g/9 oz. chestnut/cremini mushrooms, thinly sliced
- 2 garlic cloves, crushed
- a thumb-sized piece of fresh ginger, grated
- I red chilli/chile, finely chopped
- 2 shallots, finely chopped
- I lemongrass stalk, bruised and chopped
- 2 tablespoons fish sauce
- 2 tablespoons soy sauce
- I tablespoon honey
- 2 tablespoons rice vinegar
- 6 banana leaves, washed and cut into 25-cm/ 10-inch squares (or use parchment paper)
- salt

MAKES 6

Filo spinach, leek & rice pie

My childhood staple recipe. We ate this at feasts, as a snack, for breakfast, basically all the time. My grandmother always added a handful of rice to the spinach mixture to absorb the liquid after squeezing it. I was in a hurry one day and wanted to find a quicker way of absorbing the liquid, so I decided to add extra rice and loved it. It is much more substantial as a pie. So I now serve this with a salad as the main event rather than a snack.

Preheat the oven to 180°C (350°F) Gas 4. Lightly grease a 30-cm/12-inch round baking pan with 1 tablespoon olive oil and set aside.

Heat the remaining 1 tablespoon olive oil in a frying pan/skillet over a medium-high heat. Add the leeks and cook for 10 minutes or until soft. Add the spring onions/scallions, and spinach and cook until the spinach has wilted and cooked down. Remove the pan from the heat and allow to cool.

Once the spinach/leek mixture has cooled, squeeze out as much water as you can. Place in a large mixing bowl and add the rice, feta, beaten eggs and herbs and season well. Stir gently to combine.

To assemble the pie, lay one sheet of pastry on your work surface (keep the longer edge in front of you) and lightly brush with melted butter. Lay another sheet of pastry on top of the first sheet and brush with melted butter. Add enough filling to cover the width of the sheet (ie along the long edge nearest to you) and start by rolling the sheet away from you, lightly pressing, so that the filling is packed. Then roll it into a spiral and place it in the centre of your prepared baking pan. Continue in the same way, using 2 sheets of pastry at a time, brushed with the melted butter and until you have used up all of the filling. Roll each one around the previous one, to make the spiral larger.

Once you have used up all of the filling and the pan is full, brush the top with more melted butter and sprinkle with sesame seeds. Bake in the preheated oven for 45–60 minutes, or until light golden brown.

2 tablespoons olive oil
(1 for greasing the pan)

500 g/1 lb. 2 oz. leeks,
washed and sliced

1 bunch spring onions/
scallions, thinly sliced

400 g/14 oz. baby spinach

200 g/generous 1 cup short-
grain rice

300 g/10½ oz. feta cheese,
crumbled

2 eggs, beaten

15 g/½ oz. mint, leaves
picked and finely chopped

10 g/⅓ oz. dill, finely chopped

2 x 270-g/9½-oz. packs filo/
phyllo pastry

200 g/1¾ sticks butter,
melted, for brushing

2 tablespoons sesame seeds

salt and freshly ground
black pepper

SERVES 8

Braised beef with roasted carrots & mixed grains

This braised beef can be made in advance and gently reheated to serve with the roasted carrots and grains. It can be finished with Parmesan and extra basil for an Italian twist, or crumbled feta and parsley for a Greek twist. A real crowd-pleaser and simply delicious!

Heat half the oil in a heavy-based saucepan over a medium-high heat. Add the beef and cook for 2–3 minutes on each side, until nice and brown. Set aside.

Heat the remaining oil in a large saucepan on medium heat, add the onions and garlic and cook for 8–10 minutes, stirring occasionally until tender. Add the beer, sage and bay leaves, the canned cherry tomatoes with their juices, bring to a simmer, then reduce the heat to low, add beef and cook for about 3 hours, stirring occasionally, until very tender and the beef falls apart. Top up with extra beer if the mixture begins to look dry.

Meanwhile, for the roasted carrots and mixed grains, preheat the oven to 180°C (350°F) Gas 4. Combine the carrots, thyme, garlic, honey and half the oil in a roasting tray, season to taste and roast in the preheated oven for 20–25 minutes, until golden and cooked through. Set aside.

Place the burghul in a bowl, add enough boiling water to just cover and set aside for 20–30 minutes until tender and fluffy. Rinse the remaining grains separately under cold running water, drain, then cook in separate pans of boiling water until tender (15–20 minutes for barley; 10–15 minutes for quinoa and buckwheat). Drain well and set aside to cool.

To serve, combine all grains in a large bowl with the carrots, parsley, lemon juice and remaining oil. Season generously to taste and serve with the braised beef and rocket/arugula.

60 ml/¼ cup extra-virgin olive oil

800 g/1¾ lb. braising beef, cut into 3-cm/1¼-inch pieces

2 onions, finely chopped

3 garlic cloves, crushed

300 ml/1¼ cups beer, plus extra for topping up

6 sage leaves

2 bay leaves

400-g/14-oz can cherry tomatoes

100 g/3½ oz. wild rocket/ arugula (super peppery), to serve

ROASTED CARROTS & MIXED GRAINS

2 bunches heirloom carrots, trimmed and scrubbed

5 sprigs of thyme

2 garlic cloves, crushed

2 tablespoons runny honey

50 ml/3½ tablespoons extra-virgin olive oil

50 g/generous ¼ cup coarse burghul wheat

50 g/generous ¼ cup barley

50 g/generous ¼ cup red quinoa

50 g/generous ¼ cup buckwheat

20 g/¾ oz. flat-leaf parsley, leaves picked

freshly squeezed juice of 1 lemon

salt and freshly ground black pepper

SERVES 4

Crushed farro on griddled aubergine with coriander oil

Griddled aubergine/eggplant partners beautifully with the chewy, flavour-packed farro, served drizzled with a coriander/cilantro oil and a dollop of Greek yogurt on the side. This is great as part of a larger mezze table. (I have used pink amaranth leaves to garnish here too, but any combination of soft leaf herbs will work well.)

Brush each aubergine/eggplant slice with some oil, then season. Heat a griddle pan or barbecue. When hot, griddle the slices for 2–3 minutes on each side until golden brown and tender. Place the aubergine/eggplant on a serving dish while still warm and drizzle with pomegranate molasses, then cover and set aside until ready to serve.

To make the flavoured oil, blend together the coriander/cilantro and olive oil – you can do this in a jug/pitcher using a hand blender or in a free-standing blender. Set aside

For the crushed farro, rinse the farro under cold running water, then lightly pound using a mortar and pestle. Heat the oil in a large frying pan/skillet and sauté the garlic and chilli/chile for 3–4 minutes until softened. Add the farro and salt, then add the hot water, a little at a time and simmer over medium heat for 20–25 minutes, until the liquid has been absorbed and the farro is al dente. Remove from heat and stir through the rocket/arugula, if using, until wilted. Crush the farro a little more.

Uncover the aubergine/eggplant, top with the crushed farro and drizzle with the coriander/cilantro oil. Spoon over some Greek yogurt and scatter over the mixed fresh herbs to garnish.

2 aubergines/eggplants, cut into 2-cm/¾-inch slices

3 tablespoons olive oil, for brushing

2 tablespoons pomegranate molasses

Greek yogurt, to serve

CORIANDER/CILANTRO OIL

20 g/¾ oz. coriander/cilantro leaves, plus extra to garnish

80 ml/⅓ cup extra-virgin olive oil

CRUSHED FARRO

400 g/14 oz. farro

2 tablespoons olive oil

1 garlic clove, finely chopped

1 long red chilli/chile, deseeded and finely chopped

1 teaspoon salt

800 ml/scant 3½ cups hot water

30 g/1 oz. wild rocket/arugula (optional)

½ a small bunch each of coriander/cilantro, dill and parsley, leaves picked, to garnish

SERVES 4

Pan-fried mixed grain risotto with mushrooms & vermouth

Vermouth is a fortified wine flavoured with herbs, roots, bark, flowers and other botanicals and it brings an aromatic element to this dish. Using vermouth and the pre-cooked quinoa adds an earthier flavour to a classic risotto. Try cooking and freezing grains ahead so you can make multi-grain risottos like this at a moment's notice.

Soak the dried mushroom pieces in 250 ml/1 cup of the hot stock in a bowl until soft. Remove the mushrooms from the liquid and chop finely. Pour the mushroom-infused liquid back into remaining stock.

Heat 3 tablespoons olive oil and 20 g/1½ tablespoons butter in a large frying pan/skillet over a medium-high heat until the butter foams, add the portobello mushrooms and season well, then fry until tender and golden brown. Set aside.

Heat the remaining 1 tablespoon olive oil and 40 g/3 tablespoons butter in a wide saucepan over a medium heat, then add the leek, rehydrated mushrooms and garlic and sauté until translucent. Stir in the rice and thyme to coat in oil and lightly toast, then add the vermouth and stir until almost evaporated. Add the hot stock a ladleful at a time, stirring continuously until stock is absorbed before adding the next, until the rice is al dente. Add the quinoa and season to taste. Stir in the mascarpone, Parmesan, lemon zest, remaining butter and two-thirds of the portobello mushrooms. Serve topped with remaining mushrooms and extra Parmesan and chopped walnuts.

25 g/1 oz. dried mushrooms

1.5 litres/quarts vegetable stock

4 tablespoons olive oil

100 g/7 tablespoons butter, diced

500 g/1 lb. 2 oz. portobello mushrooms, thickly sliced

1 leek, halved and thinly sliced

4 garlic cloves, crushed

300 g/generous 1½ cups carnaroli rice

1 tablespoon thyme leaves

125 ml/½ cup vermouth

100 g/generous ½ cup black quinoa, cooked

120 g/4 oz. mascarpone

50 g/¾ cup finely grated Parmesan cheese (or vegetarian alternative), plus extra to serve

grated zest of 1 lemon

30 g/¼ cup toasted walnuts, chopped

salt and freshly ground black pepper

SERVES 4

Wheatberries, chorizo, orange, olive & radicchio salad

If you can get blood oranges, they look just stunning in this recipe, but if they are not in season you can use normal oranges. This is one of those dishes that looks beautiful when you bring it to the table and tastes just as good.

4 blood oranges

1 red onion, thinly sliced

2 tablespoons olive oil, plus a drizzle for frying

2 tablespoons runny honey

a pinch of dried chilli flakes/hot red pepper flakes

1 tablespoon cumin seeds, toasted

1 tablespoon coriander seeds, toasted

100 g/1 cup pitted Kalamata olives

200 g/generous 1 cup wheatberries

1 chorizo ring, chopped into discs

2 heads radicchio

20 g/¾ oz. flat-leaf parsley, leaves picked

SERVES 4

Peel and chop the oranges, and place in a serving dish. Add the sliced red onion, olive oil, honey, dried chilli flakes/hot red pepper flakes, toasted cumin and coriander seeds and black olives. Stir together and set aside to marinate for at least an hour in the serving dish.

While that all those flavours are melding, cook the wheatberries according to the package instructions, drain and add to the orange mixture while still warm – this will help all the flavours infuse more.

Heat a drizzle of oil in a large frying pan/skillet. Cook the chorizo slices for 4–5 minutes, until they are sizzling. Add to the serving dish with all the other ingredients, reserving the pan juices.

Finish with radicchio and flat-leaf parsley and serve drizzled with all the chorizo pan juices.

Wild rice & fennel with oven-roasted tomatoes & a crispy fried egg

An any-time-of-day recipe, with a combination of wild rice, fresh crispy fennel, oven-roasted tomatoes with balsamic vinegar and topped with a crispy egg. This is a great recipe to make in advance, and then top with the tomatoes and egg just before serving.

Cook the wild rice in a saucepan of boiling water for about 30 minutes until al dente or according to package instructions, then drain.

Meanwhile, preheat the oven to 180°C (350°F) Gas 4.

Place the tomatoes cut side up on a baking sheet, season with salt and pepper, then drizzle with 2 tablespoons olive oil and the balsamic vinegar. Roast in the preheated oven for 25 minutes.

In a bowl mix the cooked wild rice, with the fennel, celery, remaining olive oil, oregano, garlic, chilli/chile and lemon juice. Season to taste.

Melt the butter in a frying pan/skillet over a medium heat until frothy. Once the pan is fully heated, carefully add in the eggs, and fry until the whites are completely set but the yolks are still soft.

Divide the rice and tomatoes between 4 plates and top each with a fried egg. Add a lemon wedge on the side if you wish and enjoy.

200 g/generous 2 cups wild rice

6 small tomatoes, halved

6 tablespoons olive oil

2 tablespoons balsamic vinegar

2 baby fennel bulb with fronds, halved and thinly sliced

1 celery heart, thinly sliced

1 tablespoon finely chopped oregano

1 garlic clove, crushed

1 small red chilli/chile, finely chopped

freshly squeezed juice of 1 lemon

2 tablespoons butter

4 eggs

salt and freshly ground black pepper

lemon wedges, to serve (optional)

SERVES 4

Sweet & sour plum duck with brown rice & smashed cucumbers

This is an elegant meal with a whole range of flavours. Sweet and sour, rich and spicy and a touch of freshness from the cucumber.

For the smashed cucumber, lightly bruise the chopped cucumber in a mortar and pestle, then transfer to a bowl. Pound the garlic, ginger and sugar to a coarse paste in the mortar and pestle, add to cucumber with soy sauce and vinegar, toss to combine and refrigerate until required.

Cook the rice in a pan of boiling salted water for 12–15 minutes over a high heat until just tender, adding the peas for the last minute of cooking. Drain, refresh under cold running water, drain well and add to a large bowl.

Preheat the oven to 180°C (350°F) Gas 4. Season the duck breasts and set aside. Place the plums, with all the other ingredients in a baking dish and cook for 20 minutes. Once cooked, keep warm. Leave the oven on.

Meanwhile, continue with the rice. Add the sugar snap peas to a saucepan of boiling water and cook for 2–3 minutes, drain well and run under cold water until completely cold. Combine the soy sauce vinegar, lime juice and zest, ginger and garlic in a small bowl and leave to marinate for 10 minutes. Add the sesame oil, stir to combine, then toss through the rice mixture with spring onions/scallions and sugar snaps.

To cook the duck breasts, heat a heavy ovenproof frying pan/skillet over a medium-high heat. Place the duck in the pan, skin-side down, and cook for 5–6 minutes until the skin is golden and crisp. Tip most of the fat from the pan, then turn the duck over and sear the other side for 1 minute. Put the pan in the oven and cook for 6–8 minutes, depending on the size of the duck breasts. When ready, they should feel soft but spring back slightly when pressed. Let rest for 10 minutes before slicing to serve.

Serve the rice topped with duck slices, plums and smashed cucumber.

4 skin-on duck breasts

4 plums, halved and stoned/ pitted

a thumb-sized piece of fresh ginger, grated

2 garlic cloves, crushed

2 tablespoons apple cider vinegar

30 g/2½ tablespoons brown sugar

2 tablespoons maple syrup

3 tablespoons soy sauce

a pinch of dried chilli/hot red pepper flakes

3 star anise

1 tablespoon sesame oil

salt and freshly ground black pepper

RICE

250 g/2¼ cups brown rice

100 g/¾ cup frozen peas

100 g/generous 1 cup sugar snap peas

60 ml/¼ cup soy sauce

30 ml/2 tablespoons Chinese black vinegar

finely grated zest and freshly squeezed juice of 1 lime

a thumb-sized piece of fresh ginger, grated

1 garlic clove, finely chopped

50 ml/3½ tablespoons groundnut/peanut oil

1 teaspoon sesame oil

6 spring onions/scallions, thinly sliced diagonally

SMASHED CUCUMBER

2 Lebanese cucumbers, halved lengthways and coarsely chopped

1 garlic clove

1 tablespoon finely grated ginger

a pinch of caster/granulated sugar

2 tablespoons soy sauce

2 tablespoons rice wine vinegar

SERVES 4

Tamarind rice salad with crab & green chillies

Tamarind, with its sour-sweet tang akin to apricots and lemons, really brings this rice and green chilli/chile salad to life. The dish is full of different textures and the carmargue rice, cooling cucumber, puffed spelt, luxurious crab meat and spicy green chillies/chiles make this salad perfect for entertaining, be it a summer barbecue, a light lunch or sharing with friends.

In a serving bowl place the rice, cucumber and red onion and set aside.

Make the tamarind dressing, by mixing all the ingredients together, taste for seasoning and add 3 tablespoons water to loosen. Add to the rice mixture and set aside to infuse.

Meanwhile, preheat the oven to 180°C (350°F) Gas 4.

Place the puffed spelt and peanuts on a baking sheet and toast in the preheated oven until golden. Allow to cool.

Add the crab to the rice mixture, then top with the toasted puffed spelt and peanuts. To finish, add the herbs, green chilli/chile and spring onions/scallions. Add lime wedges for squeezing.

200 g/generous 1 cup red carmargue rice, cooked according to package instructions and cooled

1 long cucumber, halved, seeds removed and cut in half moons

½ red onion, thinly sliced

20 g/scant 1 cup puffed spelt

40 g/⅓ cup peanuts, coarsely crushed

400 g/14 oz. white crab meat

a handful each mint and coriander/cilantro, leaves picked

1 long green chilli/chile, thinly sliced diagonally

4 spring onions/scallions, thinly sliced

lime wedges, to serve

TAMARIND DRESSING

1 tablespoon tamarind paste

20 g/1 cup each mint and coriander/cilantro

1 long green chilli/chile, finely chopped

1 garlic clove, crushed

1 teaspoon ground cumin

freshly squeezed juice of 2 limes

1 teaspoon honey or to taste

3 tablespoons olive oil

2 tablespoons good-quality mayonnaise

SERVES 4 TO SHARE

My mujaddara with sour cherries

This is my take on this celebrated dish. The sour cherries with their jammy gentle tang and the lemon juice add a perfect little flavour kick. You are most welcome to leave these elements out for a more traditional approach. Try this with a simple salad or alongside some grilled meats and lemon wedges for squeezing.

Heat the 70 ml/generous ¼ cup of oil with the butter in a frying pan/skillet over a medium heat. Add the onions and stir to coat. Season with salt, then reduce heat to low and cover (use a baking sheet if you don't have a lid). Cook for about 15 minutes, stirring occasionally, until the onions are softened and translucent. (When covered, the onions steam in the liquid they release, which ensures that they'll caramelize more evenly, with less chance of burning.)

Uncover the pan and sprinkle the onions with the sugar (which increases caramelization). Increase the heat to medium-high and continue to cook the onions for 35–40 minutes until chocolatey-brown and reduced in volume by about two-thirds, stirring frequently, reducing the heat as needed and adding 1 tablespoon water to deglaze pan if it's getting too dry. Remove the onions from the pan and drain on paper towels.

Add the 1 tablespoon of oil to a large pan, add the garlic and spices and cook over medium heat for just 10–20 seconds until fragrant. Add the sour cherries, lemon juice and zest, and rice. Stir, then add the chicken stock, bring to a simmer, cover and cook for 15–20 minutes until rice is al dente.

Meanwhile, cook the green lentils in a saucepan of boiling water for 10–15 minutes until tender, then drain and set aside.

Stir the lentils through the rice during last 5 minutes of cooking and serve hot, topped with the crisp onions and with a tomato, cucumber and parsley salad and yogurt on the side.

70 ml/generous ¼ cup olive oil

40 g/3 tablespoons butter, coarsely chopped

6 onions, thinly sliced

½ teaspoon sugar

1 tablespoon oil

2 garlic cloves, finely chopped

1 teaspoon cumin seeds

1 teaspoon coriander seeds

1 cinnamon stick

½ teaspoon ground cloves

1 tablespoon ras el hanout

3 bay leaves

100 g/3½ oz. dried sour cherries

finely grated zest and freshly squeezed juice of 1 lemon

200 g/generous 1 cup long-grain rice

550 ml/2¼ cups chicken stock

200 g/generous 1 cup green lentils

salt

tomato, cucumber and parsley salad, to serve

Greek yogurt, to serve

SERVES 4

Miso brown rice salad with tofu & ginger dressing

Simplicity at best. This is a salad packed with nourishing elements that I could eat every day for lunch or dinner. It is definitely one of those dishes that you can make on a Sunday for your prep-ahead lunches. It travels well, and the miso ginger dressing all it needs for a toasty, savoury and fresh finish.

Start by making the dressing. Mix all the ingredients together and set aside.

Preheat the oven to 200°C (400°F) Gas 6.

Wrap the tofu in paper towels or a kitchen towel and place on a baking sheet. Weigh down with something heavy, like a frying pan/skillet and let it sit for 10 minutes. Unpack and unwrap tofu, then transfer to a cutting board and cut into 5-cm/2-inch cubes. Whisk together the ginger, soy sauce, white miso, and honey. Add the tofu and gently toss to coat. Sprinkle cornflour/cornstarch over and mix until incorporated. Let sit for 10 minutes.

Remove the tofu from the marinade and spread the cubes out on a baking sheet lined with parchment paper. Bake in the preheated oven for 25–30 minutes, turning halfway through, until golden brown and a thin crust forms.

Divide the rice between 2 plates, then top with edamame, sliced radishes, beetroot/beets and tofu. Drizzle with the dressing and finish with coriander/cilantro and dried chilli/hot red pepper flakes.

250 g/generous 1¼ cup brown sushi rice, cooked according to package instructions

200 g/7 oz. edamame beans

100 g/3½ oz. radishes, sliced

2 golden beetroot/beets, grated

a handful of coriander/cilantro

a pinch of dried chilli/hot red pepper flakes

DRESSING

a thumb-sized piece of fresh ginger, grated

4 spring onions/scallions, thinly sliced

3 tablespoons white miso

1 garlic clove, crushed

1 tablespoon rice vinegar

2 tablespoons sesame oil

TOFU

300-g/10½-oz. pack tofu

a thumb-sized piece of fresh ginger, grated

60 ml/¼ cup soy sauce

2 tablespoons white miso

2 tablespoons honey

1 tablespoon cornflour/cornstarch

a pinch of dried chilli/hot red pepper flakes

SERVES 2

Smoky sweet potato with seeds, grains & petimezi

Berbere is a traditional Ethiopian spice blend of chilli/chili, garlic, fenugreek and warming spices, such as cinnamon and allspice. Sweet potato is elevated by the berbere spice and alongside seeds and grains, some crème fraîche and a drizzle of petimezi (grape molasses), this appetizing dish is perfect to share.

Preheat the oven to 160°C (325°F) Gas 3.

Drizzle the whole sweet potatoes with 2 tablespoons olive oil and scatter with berbere, paprika, ground cumin, coriander and sea salt flakes. Wrap in parchment paper and then in foil and roast in the preheated oven for 35–40 minutes or until tender when pierced with a skewer. To serve, cut into quarters lengthways, then halve each crossways.

For the seeds and grains, scatter the buckwheat, sunflower seeds and pumpkin seeds on a baking sheet and roast in the preheated oven for about 10 minutes until fragrant, then add the quinoa flakes and season well with berbere and salt and pepper.

To serve, spoon crème fraîche or sour cream onto plates. Top with roasted sweet potato, scatter with seeds and grains, garnish with parsley and spring onions/scallions and drizzle with petimezi.

700 g/1½ lb. sweet potatoes

75 ml/scant ⅓ cup extra-virgin olive oil

1 teaspoon berbere (Ethiopian spice mix)

2 teaspoons smoked paprika

1 teaspoon ground cumin

1 teaspoon ground coriander

sea salt flakes

8 tablespoons crème fraîche or sour cream, to serve

flat-leaf parsley, to serve

1 bunch spring onions/scallions, thinly sliced, to serve

2 tablespoons petimezi (grape molasses), to serve

SEED & GRAINS

100 g/scant ⅔ cup buckwheat, cooked

1 teaspoon sunflower seeds

1 teaspoon pumpkin seeds

50 g/½ cup quinoa flakes

1 teaspoon berbere

salt and freshly ground black pepper

SERVES 4

Sharing
Platters

Poached trout, shaved carrot, corn & amaranth with a mustard & dill dressing

Here's a classic combination of flavours. Amaranth provides a base which is neither sweet nor savoury, but which has a subtle, slightly peppery flavour, while the delicate poached trout ramps up the nutritional value. Its looks great served on a larger platter to share or plate up individual servings, and it's gluten-free too.

Start by placing the trout fillets in a large, high-sided pan with the sliced lemon and white wine vinegar. Cover with cold water, place over a low heat and bring to a simmer. Poach for about 10 minutes, until the fish is just cooked through. Remove from the pan, allow to cool a little, then flake into large chunks.

For the dressing, whisk the mustards and sugar in a bowl to combine, then gradually add the olive oil in a thin steady stream, whisking until thick and emulsified. Whisk in the remaining ingredients and season to taste.

Meanwhile, heat a frying pan/skillet over a high heat, add 1 tablespoon olive oil, then add the corn kernels and season well. Cook for 5–6 minutes until the corn is charred and crispy. Place on a serving platter with the cooked amaranth.

Top with the remaining olive oil and season well. Add the carrots, capers, red onion and chickpea tops or herbs, then the poached trout. Serve with the mustard dill dressing drizzled over.

4 trout fillets, skin removed

1 lemon, thickly sliced

1 tablespoon white wine vinegar

2 tablespoons olive oil

3 corn cobs, kernels removed

200 g/2 cups amaranth, cooked according to package instructions

250 g/9 oz. (about 2) carrots, julienned on a mandoline

2 tablespoons capers

1 red onion, thinly sliced

salt and freshly ground black pepper

chickpea tops or other mini herbs, to garnish

MUSTARD DILL DRESSING

1 tablespoon wholegrain mustard

1 teaspoon Dijon/French mustard

2 teaspoons caster/superfine sugar

6 tablespoons olive oil

2 tablespoons freshly squeezed lemon juice, or to taste

2 tablespoons finely chopped dill

2 teaspoons jarred horseradish, or to taste

salt and freshly ground black pepper

SERVES 4–6

Harissa chicken, carrot & barley couscous

Sweet, earthy spiced chicken finished with crispy grated carrots on a bed of barley couscous. Serve straight from the tray with a crispy green salad, perfect hot or cold and great for a crowd.

Combine the chicken, harissa, lemon juice and 1 tablespoon olive oil in a bowl, season, toss to combine and leave to marinate for 10 minutes.

Heat the butter and remaining oil in a wide casserole over a medium-high heat, add the chicken skin-side down and brown well then turn over and cook for a further 15 minutes. Transfer the chicken to a plate. Add the onion, garlic and coriander seeds to the casserole and sauté until the onion is just tender. Stir in the dates, carrots, then add the barley couscous, and stir to coat in oil. Add the stock, lemon zest and hot water, season to taste, then place the chicken on top, skin-side up. Cover with a close-fitting lid, reduce the heat to very low and cook for 15 minutes, or until the chicken is cooked through and the juices run clear when pierced with the tip of a knife. Stand covered for 5 minutes

Serve with pomegranate seeds, coriander/cilantro and a crisp green salad.

8 skin-on chicken thighs, on the bone

1 tablespoon harissa

finely grated zest and freshly squeezed juice of 1 lemon

50 ml/3½ tablespoons olive oil

20 g/1½ tablespoons butter, diced

1 red onion, coarsely grated

1 garlic clove, crushed

2 teaspoons coriander seeds, crushed

6 dates, roughly chopped

2 carrots, coarsely grated

200 g/1¼ cups barley couscous

500 ml/2 cups chicken stock

185 ml/¾ cup hot water

3 tablespoons pomegranate seeds

30 g/1 oz. coriander/cilantro

salt and freshly ground black pepper

SERVES 4

Saffron pilaf

Versatile, elegant, understated and so easy. This pilaf base can work with either oven-roasted butternut squash, charred lamb cutlets or pan-fried seabass. Each recipe pairing will serve 4–6 people. See photo on pages 124–125.

Preheat the oven to 100°C (200°F) Gas ¼. Toast the saffron on a small baking sheet for just a few minutes until fragrant. Remove from the oven and increase the oven temperature to 140°C (280°F) Gas 2.

Melt the butter in a lidded casserole set over a low heat. Add the olive oil and onion and sauté until tender, then add the garlic. Add the rice and saffron, stir, then add the wine and let it bubble. Add the stock, season to taste, then bring to the boil. Add the bay leaf and cinnamon, cover and transfer to the oven. Bake for about 16–18 minutes, until the rice is tender and the stock has all been absorbed, then leave to stand for 5 minutes.

BUTTERNUT SQUASH WITH BAHARAT NUTS & SEEDS & WHIPPED RICOTTA

Preheat the oven to 180°C (350°F) Gas 4.

Place the butternut squash on a baking tray lined with parchment paper, season with salt and pepper and drizzle with olive oil and baharat spice. Roast in the preheated oven for 30 minutes.

Meanwhile, in a stand mixer with the whisk attachment, mix all the whipped ricotta ingredients for a few minutes, until light and fluffy. Set aside.

Turn the oven up to 200°C (400°F) Gas 6. Add the onions, tomatoes, chickpeas, dried chilli/hot red pepper flakes and a few tablespoons of water to the butternut squash. Roast for another 20 minute, making sure there is enough liquid in the tray. Add the seeds for the last 3 minutes. Serve on a bed of saffron pilaf alongside the whipped ricotta.

SAFFRON PILAF

½ teaspoon saffron threads

40 g/3 tablespoons unsalted butter, coarsely chopped

1 tablespoon olive oil

1 onion, finely chopped

2 garlic cloves, crushed

200 g/generous 1 cup long-grain rice, rinsed

150 ml/⅔ cup white wine

650 ml/2¾ cups chicken, fish or vegetable stock (depending on the topping)

2 small fresh bay lea leaves

2 cinnamon sticks

salt and freshly ground black pepper

BUTTERNUT SQUASH WITH BAHARAT NUTS & SEEDS

1 butternut squash, peeled and chopped into 12.5-cm/5-inch pieces

2 tablespoons olive oil, plus extra to finish

2 tablespoons baharat spice

2 red onions

300 g/10½ oz. cherry tomatoes, halved

400-g/14-oz. can chickpeas, drained

a pinch of dried chilli/hot red pepper flakes

1 tablespoon sunflower seeds

1 tablespoon pumpkin seeds

salt and freshly ground black pepper

WHIPPED RICOTTA

250 g/generous 1 cup ricotta

3 tablespoons olive oil

1 tablespoon Greek yogurt

freshly squeezed juice of 1 lemon

1 garlic clove, crushed

CHARRED LAMB CUTLETS WITH SWISS CHARD, PEAS & FETA

Take a dish large enough to accommodate the lamb cutlets in a single layer. Add the olive oil and sprinkle in the dried chilli/hot red pepper flakes, dried mint and oregano. Holding one lamb cutlet as if it were a wooden spoon, rub the oil with its sprinklings around a bit, so they are mixed, then place the lamb cutlets in a single layer, turn them instantly and leave to marinate for 10 minutes.

Meanwhile, heat a large frying pan/skillet and sauté the spring onions/ scallions for a few minutes, then add the garlic, the Swiss chard and a few tablespoons of water and allow to braise for a few minutes, Season well, then add the peas, lemon juice and feta.

Heat a griddle pan to a medium-high heat and char the lamb cutlets for a few minutes on each side. Serve with the Swiss chard mixture with mint leaves and saffron pilaf on the side.

PAN-FRIED SEA BASS WITH ASPARAGUS, SHAVED CUCUMBER & SALSA VERDE

Place the shaved asparagus on a serving platter, drizzle with lemon juice and season with salt and pepper. Set aside.

For the salsa verde, place the anchovies, capers, mustard, garlic and lemon juice in a food processor and coarsely blitz. Add the herbs and blitz further, then drizzle in the olive oil and set aside.

Season the fish with a little salt and pepper just before cooking. Heat a frying pan/skillet until very hot, then add 2 tablespoons oil. Lay the fish fillets in the pan, skin-side down. As soon as it goes in, press each fillet down with your fingers or a fish slice to stop it from curling up. Reduce the heat to medium, then leave the fish to cook for 3–4 minutes, undisturbed, until you can see that the flesh has cooked two-thirds of the way up and the skin is crisp and brown. Flip the fillets over, then fry on the flesh side for about 2 minutes until just done, basting the skin with the oil in the pan as it cooks.

Add the cucumber to serving dish with the asparagus and the lamb's lettuce. Add the dry roasted grains and top with the cooked sea bass. Drizzle with the salsa verde and serve alongside the saffron pilaf.

CHARRED LAMB CUTLETS

8 lamb cutlets

2 tablespoons olive oil

a pinch of dried chilli/hot red pepper flakes

1 teaspoon dried mint

1 teaspoon dried oregano

SWISS CHARD PEAS & FETA

1 bunch spring onions/ scallions

1 garlic clove, crushed

2 bunches Swiss chard, roughly chopped

300 g/2¼ cups frozen peas, defrosted

freshly squeezed juice of 1 lemon

200 g/7 oz. feta cheese, crumbled

30 g/1 oz. mint, leaves picked

PAN-FRIED SEA BASS WITH ASPARAGUS & SHAVED CUCUMBER

1 bunch asparagus, shaved

freshly squeezed juice of 1 lemon

4 fillets sea bass (skin-on)

2 tablespoons olive oil

2 Lebanese cucumbers, shaved

100 g/3½ oz. lamb's lettuce

100 g/generous ½ cup dry roasted mixed grains

salt and freshly ground black pepper

SALSA VERDE

4 canned anchovies

2 tablespoons capers, chopped

1 tablespoon wholegrain mustard

1 garlic clove, crushed

freshly squeezed juice of 1 lemon

30 g/1 oz. flat-leaf parsley

20 g/¾ oz. basil

6 tablespoons olive oil

Black bean rice with slow-cooked pork

This is a simple, satisfying rice dish bursting with Latin flavours of garlic, oregano and cumin and a squeeze of orange. Perfect with the slow-cooked pork.

Preheat the oven to 220°C (425°F) Gas 7. Place the pork shoulder in a deep-sided baking dish and tuck the onion wedges underneath it. Drizzle the pork skin with a little olive oil, then massage 1 tablespoon of salt into the skin, forcing it into the score marks. Cook in the preheated oven for 30 minutes or until the crackling is crisp and golden-brown.

In a bowl mix the habanero chilli/chili sauce, ground cumin, coffee and maple syrup and rub all over the crackling. Then pour the canned tomatoes, chicken stock, ancho chillies/chiles and half the orange juice into the baking dish, add the bay leaves and place back into the oven. Turn the oven down to 180°C (350°F) Gas 4. Cook for 30 minutes per 500 g/1 lb. 2 oz., or until the pork is cooked through (the juices will run clear when pierced with a knife) – this will take approx 2½–3 hours. Add more water if the sauce cooks down too much, it should be thick and rich.

Meanwhile, cook the rice. Heat the olive oil in a saucepan over a medium-high heat, add the onion and garlic and sauté until tender. Add the rice, stir to coat, then add the stock, dried oregano, ground cumin, chilli/hot red pepper flakes and remaining orange juice and season to taste. Bring to the boil, then reduce the heat to medium, cover with a tight-fitting lid and cook for 15–20 minutes until the rice is tender and liquid is absorbed. Add the beans, coriander/cilantro, lime juice and zest, and extra-virgin olive oil.

When the pork is cooked remove it from the baking dish and rest it for 20 minutes, covered, then shred the meat with 2 forks and mix in with the sauce. Serve the rice hot with the pulled pork, topped with coriander/cilantro and jalapeños, and with lime wedges alongside.

2 tablespoons olive oil

1 onion, finely chopped

1 garlic clove, finely chopped

200 g/generous 1 cup long-grain white rice

700 ml/scant 3 cups chicken stock (stock cube is fine)

400-g/14-oz. can black beans, drained and rinsed

30 g/1 oz. coriander/cilantro, plus extra to serve

1½ tablespoons extra-virgin olive oil

grated zest and freshly squeezed juice of 2 limes

salt and freshly ground black pepper

1 teaspoon dried oregano

1 teaspoon ground cumin

a pinch of dried chilli/hot red pepper flakes

freshly squeezed juice of 1 orange (half for the rice, half for the pork)

pickled jalapeño chillies/chiles, coarsely chopped, to serve

SLOW-COOKED PORK

1.7 kg/3¾ lb. rolled pork shoulder/Boston butt, skin scored

1 onion, cut into wedges

2 tablespoons olive oil

1 tablespoon habanero chilli/chili sauce

1 tablespoon ground cumin

1 tablespoon instant coffee granules

1 tablespoon maple syrup

400-g/14-oz. can crushed tomatoes

500 ml/2 cups chicken stock

2 large ancho chillies/chiles, rehydrated

reserved orange juice (see above)

2 fresh bay leaves

salt

SERVES 4

Biriyani for a crowd with fresh mango relish

Here is a vegan update of this regal dish, made by layering the marinated aubergine/eggplant with rice, saffron and spices. So full of flavour and depth, this is a dish that never disappoints.

Cut the aubergines/eggplants into 2-cm/¾-inch chunks. Place all the marinade ingredients in a bowl, mix together, then add the aubergine chunks and refrigerate, covered, overnight (or for a minimum of 1 hour).

Meanwhile, wash the rice in a couple of changes of water, then soak it in a bowl of water for 20 minutes. Bring 2.5 litres/quarts of water to the boil in a large saucepan. Add the drained rice, lime juice and ½ teaspoon salt and boil for 6 minutes, until the rice is two-thirds cooked. Drain the rice and spread it out on a tray to cool.

In a high-sided pan (with a lid), heat 2 tablespoons of the coconut oil and fry the aubergine/eggplant for about 6 minutes until soft, cooked through and golden on all sides. Transfer to a plate. Reserve the marinade for later.

Fry the onion in the remaining oil in the high-sided pan until soft and lightly browned. Add a pinch of salt, garlic, chillies/chiles, cumin seeds, cardamom and cinnamon and cook for a few minutes until fragrant. Then add the tomato purée/paste, soy sauce, curry leaves, bay leaves and garam masala and cook for a further minute. Add the rice, aubergine/eggplant and reserved marinade back to the pan. Mix the stock cube in 500 ml/2 cups water, then add to the pan, along with the chickpeas, and mix thoroughly. Top the rice with the saffron and water mixture, walnuts, raisins, barbaries and pistachios. Cover and cook on low-medium heat for 30 minutes, making sure that there is enough liquid (add a little more water if the pan is looking dry). Meanwhile, make the mango relish by mixing all the ingredients together in a bowl and checking the seasoning.

Serve the biriyani topped with the fresh mango relish and some plant-based yogurt mixed with some chopped fresh herbs.

3 aubergines/eggplants
500 g/2 cups basmati rice
freshly squeezed juice of 1 lime
3 tablespoons coconut oil
2 onions, thinly sliced
2 garlic cloves, crushed
2 green chillies/chiles, sliced
2 teaspoons cumin seeds
8 cardamom pods, bruised
1 cinnamon stick
1 tablespoon tomato purée/paste
1 tablespoon soy sauce
1–2 sprigs curry leaves
3 bay leaves
1 tablespoon garam masala
1 vegetable stock cube
400-g/14-oz. can chickpeas, rinsed and drained
½ teaspoon saffron strands, soaked in 120 ml/½ cup warm water
30 g/¼ cup walnuts, toasted
30 g/¼ cup raisins
30 g/¼ cup barberries or sour cherries
30 g/¼ cup pistachios, toasted
sea salt
plant-based yogurt, to serve

MARINADE
1 garlic clove, crushed
a thumb-sized piece of fresh ginger, grated
400-g/14-oz. can coconut milk
½ teaspoon ground turmeric
1 teaspoon chilli/chili powder
freshly squeezed juice of 1 lemon

FRESH MANGO RELISH
1 mango, diced
1 red onion, diced
freshly squeezed juice of 1 lime
1 red chilli/chile, chopped
¼ bunch coriander/cilantro, chopped
¼ bunch mint, leaves picked

SERVES 6–8

Buckwheat tabbouleh with beans & grainy lamb meatballs

Using buckwheat in this mixed bean tabbouleh makes it a great gluten-free alternative. Buckwheat also has a high antioxidant and mineral content. This can be a great sharing salad with the grainy lamb meatballs, or part of a larger sharing table with the addition of other elements. Roasting the garlic in the dressing makes it more mellow and just delicious.

Start by making roast garlic dressing. Preheat the oven to 200°C (400°F) Gas 6. Wrap the garlic tightly in foil, place on a baking sheet and roast for 30–35 minutes until tender and caramelized. When cool enough to handle, squeeze the garlic from skins into a bowl (discard the skins), whisk in the oil, lemon juice and zest, and sumac, season to taste and set aside.

To make the meatballs, add the burghul, lamb, garlic, spices and a pinch each of salt and pepper to a food processor and pulse to combine well. With slightly wet hands, shape the lamb mixture into golf ball-sized balls, then massage them a little to create elasticity, and shape into ovals. Place on a tray and refrigerate until required.

Fry the meatballs for 8–10 minutes (in two batches), turning occasionally, until golden and cooked through. Keep warm.

To make the tabbouleh, combine the buckwheat, beans, peas, pumpkin seeds and herbs in a bowl, drizzle with dressing, season to taste and toss to combine. Scatter the red onion and pine nuts over the top.

Serve the tabbouleh with meatballs, with pita breads sprinkled with sumac on the side.

150 g/scant 1 cup buckwheat, cooked and cooled

400-g/14-oz. can butterbeans/lima beans

200 g/1½ cups broad/fava beans, skins removed

200 g/1½ cups frozen peas, blanched and refreshed

100 g/3½ oz. mixed fine green beans, blanched and refreshed

30 g/¼ cup toasted pumpkin seeds

1 bunch flat-leaf parsley, finely chopped

1 bunch mint, leaves picked and finely chopped

½ red onion, thinly sliced

30 g/2 tablespoons pickled red chillies/chiles, chopped (optional)

2 tablespoons toasted pine nuts

ROAST GARLIC DRESSING

1 bulb garlic

60 ml/¼ cup extra-virgin olive oil

finely grated zest and freshly squeezed juice of 2 lemons

1 teaspoon sumac

GRAINY LAMB MEATBALLS

75 g/scant ½ cup burghul, soaked overnight in water in the fridge

500 g/1 lb. 2 oz. minced/ground lamb

2 garlic cloves, crushed

2 teaspoons paprika

½ teaspoon ground cloves

½ teaspoon ground cinnamon

salt and freshly ground black pepper

vegetable oil, for shallow-frying

TO SERVE

warmed pita breads

sumac, to sprinkle

SERVES 4

Spatchcocked bbq chicken with rice & peas & charred pineapple

This earthy, spicy jerk-flavoured chicken pairs so well with rice and peas, which combine with a mixture of citrus juice and zest and coconut milk. If there are any leftovers, I shred the chicken, chop the pineapple and add to the rice and peas for a cold salad.

Start the chicken the day before. Process the bay leaves, spring onions/scallions, chilli/chile, thyme, spices and 1 teaspoon sea salt in a food processor until finely chopped. Add the soy sauce, sugar and lime juice and zest and process to combine. Rub the paste all over the chicken, then marinate overnight in an airtight container in the fridge.

For the rice and peas, bring the coconut milk, stock, chilli/chile and 1 teaspoon sea salt to the boil in a saucepan over a medium-high heat, then add the rice, stir to combine and return to the boil. Reduce the heat to low and simmer for 25–30 minutes until tender. Remove from heat, stand for 10 minutes, then strain off any excess liquid. Discard the chilli/chile and spread the rice out on a tray for 1 hour to cool to room temperature. Meanwhile, blanch the peas for 1–2 minutes until tender, drain and refresh in cold water, then place in a bowl with cooled rice, spring onions/scallions, oil, lime and orange juice and zest. Season to taste, stir to combine and refrigerate until required.

Heat a barbecue to medium. Wipe excess marinade from the chicken and drizzle with a little oil. Cook for 5 minutes each side in the centre of the grill, then draw aside to the edges to cook on a gentler heat, turning regularly. To check that it is cooked through, pierce with a knife between the thighs and the breast bone, the flesh should be white and firm.

To make the charred pineapple, place all the ingredients in a bowl and mix well to combine. Cook the pineapple on the barbecue for 2–3 minutes on each side, or until lightly charred.

Serve the chicken hot with rice and peas, pineapple and lime wedges.

6 fresh bay leaves, torn

4 spring onions/scallions (including half the green parts), coarsely chopped

3 habanero chillies/chiles, coarsely chopped

6 sprigs of thyme, leaves picked

2 teaspoons ground allspice

2 teaspoons freshly ground peppercorns

1 teaspoon ground cinnamon

freshly ground nutmeg

2 tablespoons soy sauce

1 tablespoon brown sugar

freshly squeezed juice and finely grated zest of 1 lime

1 chicken, spatchcocked

salt

lime wedges, to serve

RICE & PEAS

400-g/14-oz. can coconut milk

500 ml/2 cups chicken stock

1 habanero chilli/chile, halved

1 teaspoon sea salt

200 g/generous 1 cup long-grain rice

200 g/1½ cups frozen peas

1 bunch spring onions/scallions, thinly sliced

2 tablespoons olive oil

finely grated zest and freshly squeezed juice of 1 lime and 1 orange

salt and freshly ground black pepper

CHARRED PINEAPPLE

1 pineapple, peeled and cut into wedges

50 g/3½ tablespoons butter

1 tablespoon brown sugar

½ teaspoon cayenne pepper

freshly squeezed juice of 1 lime

SERVES 4

Insalata primavera with grains, goat's cheese & fresh mint dressing

Primavera means spring in Italian and this dish is the epitome of spring. It is perfect to share, as a side to a pasta dish or to accompany a barbecue. The mixture of spring vegetables – asparagus, courgettes/zucchini and broad/fava beans – fresh goat's cheese and a minty dressing results in a salad that you will make time and time again.

For the mint dressing, mix the ingredients together in a bowl and season to taste.

Combine the quinoa, asparagus, courgette/zucchini, broad/fava beans, spring onions/scallions, parsley and chives in a large bowl, drizzle with the mint dressing to taste and toss lightly to combine.

Scatter with soft salad leaves and goat's cheese, then drizzle with extra dressing and serve.

200 g/generous 1 cup quinoa, cooked according to package instructions

2 bunches asparagus, trimmed and thinly sliced lengthways on a mandoline

3 courgettes/zucchini, thinly sliced lengthways on a mandoline

300 g/1½ cups shelled broad/fava beans, peeled

1 bunch spring onions/scallions, thinly sliced

a small handful of parsley and a few chives, finely chopped

150 g/5½ oz. soft salad leaves

200 g/7 oz. soft goat's cheese, crumbled

FRESH MINT DRESSING

100 ml/scant ½ cup extra-virgin olive oil

30 g/1 oz. mint, leaves picked and finely chopped

finely grated zest and freshly squeezed juice of 1 lemon

1 tablespoon apple cider vinegar

1 garlic clove, crushed

a pinch of sugar

salt and freshly ground black pepper

SERVES 4

Sweet Things

Peach, quinoa & almond cakes

If you thought quinoa was just for salads, think again! These light and fluffy dessert cakes make a delightful change to using the more familiar polenta. A batter containing ground almonds and peach purée keeps things moist, while sweet dessert wine adds a touch of decadence to the roasted peaches in syrup.

Preheat the oven to 200°C (400°F) Gas 6. Scatter 170 g/generous ¾ cup of the sugar in the base of a roasting pan large enough to hold the peaches snugly in a single layer. Arrange them cut-side down in the pan, pressing them into the sugar, then turn them over so the cut sides face up.

In a jug/cup mix the dessert wine, lemon juice, zest and 1 teaspoon vanilla paste and drizzle over the peaches. Roast the peaches in the preheated oven for 20–25 minutes until golden and tender, spooning the pan juices over peaches a few times during cooking. Transfer half the peaches and 50 ml/3½ tablespoons of the pan juices to a food processor, process to a purée and set aside. Reserve the rest of the peaches and juices.

Place the quinoa, remaining vanilla paste and 300 ml/1¼ cups water in a saucepan and bring to the boil over a medium-high heat, reduce the heat to medium and simmer for 12–15 minutes until the liquid evaporates and quinoa is tender. Drain through a fine sieve/strainer to remove any remaining liquid, then spread on a tray to cool and dry.

Preheat the oven to 180°C (350°F) Gas 4. Whisk the eggs and remaining sugar in an electric mixer for 6–8 minutes until pale and fluffy, add the butter and whisk to combine. Sift over the flour and baking powder, stir to combine, stir in the peach purée, ground almonds and quinoa, then spoon into the 12 prepared moulds, smoothing the tops. Scatter with almonds. Bake in the preheated oven for 20–25 minutes until the cakes are golden and the centres spring back when lightly pressed. Let cool in the moulds for 10 minutes, then turn onto a wire rack. Serve warm or at room temperature with roast peaches, syrup and extra flaked almonds.

500 g/2½ cups raw caster/superfine sugar

6 peaches, quartered, stones/pits removed

4 tablespoons dessert wine

finely grated zest and freshly squeezed juice of 1 lemon

2 teaspoons vanilla paste

90 g/½ cup white quinoa, rinsed

4 eggs

200 g/1¾ sticks butter, melted and cooled

200 g/1½ cups plain/all-purpose flour

1 teaspoon baking powder

70 g/⅔ cup ground almonds

60 g/¾ cup flaked/slivered almonds, plus extra for serving

12 x 150-ml/⅔-cup capacity metal dariole moulds, buttered and floured

MAKES 12 SMALL CAKES

Oat & honey cake with whipped tahini & honey frosting

A winning combination of oats, honey, walnuts and spices, this cake will become your family's go-to for elevenses, afternoon tea or as a dessert. The tahini and honey buttercream frosting is the perfect finishing touch – the tahini adds just a hint of sesame and is rounded off with a drizzle of honey.

Preheat the oven to 180°C (350°F) Gas 4. Grease and base-line 2 x 20-cm/8-inch sandwich pans.

For the cake, in a stand mixer, mix the butter, sugar and honey until light and fluffy and start adding the beaten eggs little by little. Once fully incorporated, add the flour, oats, carrot, walnuts, sultanas/golden raisins, cinnamon, nutmeg, lemon zest and juice, and mix together.

Pour into the prepared cake pans and bake in the preheated oven for 20–25 minutes, or until golden and a skewer inserted in the centre comes out clean. Allow the cakes to cool in the pan for 10 minutes, then turn out onto a wire rack to fully cool.

Meanwhile, make the frosting. Beat the butter until soft. Add half the icing/confectioners' sugar and continue to beat until well combined. Add the remaining icing/confectioners' sugar and beat again. When the frosting is smooth, add the tahini and vanilla extract and beat again until well combined and fluffy.

Use a sharp knife to level the top of each cake so they are even. Place one of the cakes on a cake stand or board and spread with a third of the frosting, making sure it goes all the way to the edges. Place the second cake on top and cover the top with the remaining frosting. Drizzle with honey, decorate with edible flowers, if using, and serve.

300 g/2¾ sticks butter
150 g/¾ cup light muscovado sugar
100 g/6 tablespoons honey
4 eggs, beaten
100 g/1 cup jumbo rolled/old-fashioned oats
300 g/2¼ cups self-raising/self-rising flour
200 g/7 oz. carrot, grated (1 large carrot)
50 g/⅓ cup walnuts, chopped
50 g/⅓ cup sultanas/golden raisins
1 teaspoon ground cinnamon
1 teaspoon freshly ground nutmeg
finely grated zest and freshly squeezed juice of 1 lemon

FROSTING
250 g/2¼ sticks butter
300 g/generous 2 cups icing/confectioners' sugar
30 g/2½ tablespoons tahini (or more to taste)
1 teaspoon vanilla extract

TO FINISH
50 g/3 tablespoons honey
edible flowers, to decorate (optional)

SERVES 6

Rice fritters with vanilla & orange blossom cream

In Italy these are called *frittelle di riso*. This version has a dash of rum in the mixture and dipped into a vanilla and orange blossom cream. Serve with a shot of espresso at the end of the meal, or in a bowl with a scoop of ice cream when you are feeling decadent.

Place the milk, rice, butter, vanilla pod/bean and seeds and orange zest in a saucepan and bring to the boil over a medium heat, reduce the heat to low and simmer for 20–25 minutes, stirring occasionally, until the rice is tender. Transfer to a bowl, cool to room temperature and discard the vanilla pod/bean. Add the flour, sugar, eggs, bicarbonate of soda/baking soda and rum to the cooled mixture, stir to combine and refrigerate until firm.

Meanwhile, for the vanilla and orange blossom cream, place all the ingredients into a mixer and mix together. Spoon into a serving bowl and set aside in the fridge.

For the vanilla sugar, combine the ingredients in a bowl and set aside.

Heat the vegetable oil in a large saucepan over a medium heat to 180°C (350°F). Deep-fry tablespoons of the mixture in batches for 2–3 minutes, turning occasionally, until golden and cooked through. Drain on paper towels, sprinkle with the vanilla sugar and serve hot with a spoonful of the vanilla and orange blossom cream on the side.

500 ml/2 cups rice milk

250 g/1⅓ cups arborio rice

30 g/2 tablespoons unsalted butter, coarsely chopped

I vanilla pod/bean, split and seeds scraped

finely grated zest of I orange

140 g/I cup plain/all-purpose flour

100 g/½ cup caster/granulated sugar

2 eggs, lightly beaten

½ teaspoon bicarbonate of soda/baking soda

25 ml/5 teaspoons dark rum

vegetable oil, for deep-frying

VANILLA & ORANGE BLOSSOM CREAM

100 ml/scant ½ cup double/heavy cream

150 g/5½ oz. mascarpone

I teaspoon vanilla paste

50 g/5 tablespoon icing/confectioners' sugar

I teaspoon orange blossom water

VANILLA SUGAR

150 g/¾ cup caster/granulated sugar

I teaspoon powdered vanilla

SERVES 4

Simple creamy rice pudding with seasonal toppings

This rich, creamy rice is great served warm with your choice of topping, but is also lovely chilled and set.

Heat the milk, cream, vanilla pod/bean and seeds and half the sugar in a large heavy-based saucepan over a medium heat, stirring to dissolve the sugar. Add the rice and bring to the boil, then reduce the heat to low and cook for 15–20 minutes, stirring occasionally until thick and the rice is tender.

Whisk the egg yolks and the remaining sugar in a bowl until thick and pale. Remove the rice mixture from the heat and whisk in the egg mixture. Return the pan to the heat and lightly cook the eggs for 5 minutes, stirring continuously. Remove from the heat, set aside and keep warm.

CHERRY & RHUBARB TOPPING

Put the rhubarb into a saucepan with the sugar and 300 ml/1¼ cups water. Bring to the boil, then reduce the heat and simmer for 8 minutes until the rhubarb is cooked but still holds its shape. Add the cherries, just to soften. Top each bowl of rice pudding with this mixture and add a few fresh cherries to serve.

SPICED APPLE TOPPING

Put the apples in a saucepan with the cinnamon, raisins, nutmeg, cloves, star anise and cardamom pods and 2 tablespoons of water. Bring to a simmer, then cover and cook for 10–15 minutes until the apples are very soft. Top each bowl of rice pudding with this mixture, and drizzle with maple syrup to serve.

800 ml/scant 3½ cups milk

400 ml/1¾ cups double/heavy cream

1 vanilla pod/bean, split and seeds scraped

150 g/¾ cup light soft brown sugar

250 g/generous ¼ cups short-grain pudding rice

2 egg yolks

2 orange rinds

2 tablespoons brandy

1 bay leaf

CHERRY RHUBARB TOPPING (FOR SPRING & SUMMER)

200 g/7 oz. rhubarb, cut into 2.5-cm/1-inch pieces

200 g/7 oz. cherries, halved and stoned/pitted (reserve a few whole to serve)

100 g/½ cup caster/granulated sugar

SPICED APPLE TOPPING (FOR AUTUMN/FALL & WINTER)

4 Granny Smith apples, peeled, cored and chopped

1 teaspoon ground cinnamon

50 g/scant ⅓ cup raisins

freshly grated nutmeg

4 cloves

1 star anise

3 cardamom pods, bruised

maple syrup, to finish

SERVES 4–6

Chocolate rye cookies

An elegant, grown-up cookie with the addition of dark rye flour and delicious studs of melting dark chocolate. Very moreish!

In a stand mixer, cream the butter and sugar until light and fluffy. Add the baking powder and salt and mix for another minute. Add the egg and vanilla seeds and mix to combine. Add the rye flour and gently mix until a uniform dough forms, then mix in the chocolate chips until well distributed. Flatten the dough into a disc, cover with clingfilm/plastic wrap and refrigerate for at least 20 minutes.

When ready to bake, preheat the oven to 180°C (350°F) Gas 4.

Divide the dough into 16 portions, rolling each into a ball. Place on parchment-lined baking sheets at least 7.5 cm/3 inches apart. Bake in the preheated oven for 16 minutes, turning the baking sheets halfway through for an even bake.

Allow to cool completely on a wire rack before serving. Store in an airtight container for up to 3 days.

120 g/9 tablespoons unsalted butter

200 g/1 cup golden caster/ granulated sugar

½ teaspoon baking powder

a pinch of sea salt

1 large/US extra-large egg

seeds of 1 vanilla pod/bean

160 g/1½ cups dark rye flour

180 g/generous 1 cup dark/ bittersweet chocolate chips

MAKES 16

Coconut chocolate traybake

This is a lovely coconut and dark chocolate delight. It is vegan and gluten-free, with a base of dates, cashew nut butter, coconut, oats and puffed rice. A very versatile traybake.

Preheat the oven to 160°C (325°F) Gas 3.

Add the dates and maple syrup to a food processor and pulse a few times to chop, without forming a ball. Add the cashews, desiccated/dried shredded coconut, coconut oil, cashew nut butter and 100 ml/scant ½ cup water. Process until the ingredients are well mixed and stick together when pressed, then add the oats, puffed rice and salt and blitz once or twice trying to keep the texture as much as possible.

Transfer to a 23-cm/9-inch square dish and press down in an even layer. Bake in the preheated oven for 10 minutes, then set aside to cool.

Melt the chocolate by placing it in a bowl and melting it in a microwave for about 2 minutes (or place in a bowl set over a pan of gently simmering water). You can add a teaspoon of coconut oil if desired to help melt. Pour the chocolate over the traybake and spread it evenly. Top with coconut flakes immediately before the chocolate hardens to make sure they stick.

Place the traybake in the fridge or freezer for the chocolate to harden, then cut into bars and enjoy!

200 g/7 oz. Medjool dates, stoned/pitted

100 ml/scant ½ cup maple syrup

200 g/1⅔ cups raw cashews

100 g/1¼ cups desiccated/dried unsweetened shredded coconut

4 tablespoons coconut oil

3 tablespoons cashew nut butter

100 g/1 cup gluten-free rolled/old-fashioned oats

100 g/4 cups puffed rice

a pinch of salt

CHOCOLATE TOPPING

300 g/10½ oz. dark/bittersweet chocolate

1 teaspoon coconut oil (optional)

coconut flakes, to decorate

SERVES 8 OR MORE

Black coconut quinoa with griddled mango & makrut lime syrup

This is one of those super-versatile recipes that could be served at breakfast, brunch or even as a dessert. For dessert it's great with some ice cream and toasted coconut.

Rinse the quinoa under cold running water, place in a saucepan and cover generously with cold water. Bring to the boil over a medium-high heat and cook for about 10 minutes, or until tender. Drain well, then set aside to cool slightly.

Meanwhile, for the makrut lime syrup, stir the sugar, lime juice and zest and 150 ml/⅔ cup water together in a saucepan over a medium heat to dissolve the sugar, then simmer until combined. Remove from the heat, add the makrut lime leaves and set aside to infuse for 1 hour, then strain into a jug/pitcher.

Heat a griddle pan over a high heat. Sprinkle the mango halves with palm sugar/jaggery and griddle/grill for a few minutes. All you want to do is char and caramelize the mango for flavour, not cook all the way through.

In another saucepan gently heat the coconut cream with the palm sugar/jaggery, makrut lime leaves, and lemongrass stalk, then add the quinoa and heat through. Remove and discard the lime leaves and lemongrass stalk.

Divide among serving bowls, top with griddled mango, drizzle with the syrup to taste (serving any extra syrup on the side) and garnish with edible flowers, if liked.

200 g/generous 1 cup black quinoa

300 ml/1¼ cups coconut cream

80 g/3 oz. palm sugar/jaggery

3 makrut lime leaves

1 lemongrass stalk, bashed

edible flowers, to garnish (optional)

MAKRUT LIME SYRUP

100 g/½ cup caster/granulated sugar

finely grated zest and freshly squeezed juice of 4 limes

20 makrut lime leaves, coarsely torn

GRIDDLED MANGO

2 firm mangoes, halved

2 tablespoons palm sugar/jaggery

SERVES 4

Lemon cheesecake with sour cream topping & strawberries in limoncello

Everyone should have a good baked cheesecake in their recipe arsenal. This is one of those recipes. The base is made with a combination of oats and quinoa flakes with some honey and butter. The filling has a combination of lemon and limoncello topped with strawberries for extra freshness. In autumn/fall and winter you can use frozen berries, gently poached with a little limoncello and a drizzle of honey, as an alternative topping.

Preheat the oven to 180°C (350°F) Gas 4.

Melt the butter and honey together in a saucepan over a gentle heat, then stir in the oats and quinoa. Press the mixture into a 20-cm/8-inch round loose-bottomed cake pan and set aside.

For the filling, process the cream cheese in a food processor until smooth, then add the eggs and pulse until just combined. Add the cream, sugar and lemon zest and process until combined. Add a pinch of salt then, with the motor running, gradually add the lemon juice and process until just combined. Gently mix through the limoncello and pour the mixture on to the base.

Reduce the oven to 150°C (300°F) Gas 2 and bake for 30–35 minutes until the cheesecake is just set, with only a slight wobble in the centre when you shake the pan. Set aside for 20–25 minutes to cool, then refrigerate for 2½–3 hours until chilled and firm.

For the sour cream topping, swirl the lemon curd through the sour cream. Hull the strawberries and drizzle with limoncello. Top the cheesecake with the swirled sour cream and strawberries and a few edible flowers, if using and serve.

BASE

100 g/7 tablespoons butter

70 g/¼ cup honey

20 g/scant ¼ cup rolled/old-fashioned oats

100 g/1 cup quinoa flakes

FILLING

400 g/14 oz. full-fat cream cheese, softened

3 eggs

400 ml/1¾ cups double/heavy cream

50 g/scant ¼ cup acacia honey

50 g/¼ cup caster/superfine sugar

finely grated zest and freshly squeezed juice of 2 lemons

a pinch of salt

2 tablespoons limoncello

TOPPING

100 g/⅓ cup lemon curd

100 g/scant ½ cup sour cream

200 g/2 cups strawberries

1–2 tablespoons limoncello

edible flowers, to garnish (optional)

SERVES 6

Olive oil, lime &
pistachio polenta cake

This cake is moist, delicate, light, gently nutty and zesty all at the same time. It is the perfect tea cake, or serve as a dessert with a dollop of Greek yogurt on the side. The olive oil pairs very well with the lime and pistachio and makes for a very moist crumb.

Preheat the oven to 160°C (325°F) Gas 3 and grease a 23-cm/9-inch springform cake pan.

Put the pistachios in a food processor and blend to a fine powder.

Melt the butter gently in a pan and add to the olive oil. Whisk the eggs and sugar together until light and fluffy. Slowly add the butter and oil mixture into the whisked egg mixture a little at a time with the whisk on a low speed until you have a thick emulsion.

Sift the flour, then whisk the flour, polenta/cornmeal, baking powder and ground pistachios into the egg mixture. Fold the lime juice and zest into the mixture.

Add the mixture into the prepared cake pan and bake in the middle of the preheated oven for 50 minutes. Insert a skewer into the centre of the cake and when it comes out clean, the cake is cooked. Leave the cake to rest in the cake pan for 10 minutes, then turn out and cool on a wire rack.

Dust with icing/confectioners' sugar and sprinkle over the chopped pistachios. Serve with a dollop of Greek yogurt on the side, if liked.

200 g/1⅔ cups pistachio nuts, shelled and chopped, plus extra to decorate

100 g/7 tablespoons butter, plus extra for greasing

100 ml/scant ½ cup unfiltered extra virgin olive oil

3 eggs

200 g/1 cup golden caster/granulated sugar

50 g/6 tablespoons plain/all-purpose flour

50 g/⅓ cup finely ground polenta/cornmeal

1 teaspoon baking powder

finely grated zest and freshly squeezed juice of 3 limes

icing/confectioners' sugar, for dusting

Greek yogurt, to serve (optional)

SERVES 8

Sweet rice pie

An indulgent sweet rice pie for a celebration, this recipe is based on a Neapolitan Easter rice pie. Rice pudding mingles with chocolate, orange and chopped hazelnuts for a perfect end to a long lunch or dinner party. If you have left over rice pudding, you can use that and add the flavourings.

To make the pastry, process the flour, sugar and salt in a food processor to combine. Add the butter, process until the mixture resembles fine crumbs, then add the egg yolks and process to combine. Turn onto a lightly floured surface, bring together with the heel of your hand, wrap in clingfilm/plastic wrap and refrigerate for 1 hour to rest.

Roll out the pastry on a lightly floured surface to 3 mm/⅛ inch thick. Line a 23-cm/9-inch tart pan, trim the edges and refrigerate for 1 hour.

Meanwhile, for the filling, bring the milk, cream, rice and vanilla paste to the boil in a saucepan over a medium-high heat, then reduce the heat to medium and simmer for 15–20 minutes, stirring occasionally, until the liquid is absorbed and the rice is tender.

Preheat the oven to 180°C (350°F) Gas 4.

Whisk the egg yolks, orange zest, 80 g/scant ½ cup sugar and half the butter in a bowl to combine. Stir into the rice mixture and set aside to cool slightly. Stir in the chocolate and hazelnuts. Spoon into the pastry case, filling to 5 mm/¼ inch below the rim and set aside.

Whisk the whole egg, spices, remaining butter and remaining sugar in a separate bowl, and drizzle over the rice mixture. Bake in the preheated oven for 45–60 minutes until golden and firm to touch (cover with foil if it too quickly). Remove from the oven and leave to stand for 15 minutes.

To serve, top with the grated chocolate, hazelnuts and orange zest, then dust with icing/confectioners' sugar. If the pie has been refrigerated, bring to room temperature before serving.

450 ml/scant 2 cups milk

300 ml/1¼ cups double/heavy cream

160 g/generous ¾ cup arborio rice

1 teaspoon vanilla paste

4 egg yolks

finely grated zest of 1 orange

100 g/½ cup raw cane sugar (rapadura)

100 g/7 tablespoons butter, melted and cooled

90 g/3 oz. dark/bittersweet chocolate, chopped

50 g/generous ⅓ cup hazelnuts, chopped, plus extra to decorate

1 egg

freshly grated nutmeg

1 teaspoon ground cinnamon

PASTRY

250 g/scant 2 cups plain/all-purpose flour

60 g/generous ¼ cup caster/granulated sugar

a pinch of salt

120 g/1 stick cold butter, coarsely chopped

3 egg yolks

TO FINISH

grated chocolate

icing/confectioners' sugar

grated zest of 1 orange

SERVES 8

Index

Acknowledgements

FROM THE AUTHOR

Just a few very simple words that mean so much. Thank you to all the extended team at RPS, Cindy Richards, Leslie Harrington, Julia Charles, Megan Smith, Gillian Haslam, Patricia Harrington, Gordana Simakovic and Hilary Bird. Without you this book would not be possible – thank you for your guidance and for letting me present recipes to share with the world of food lovers. It never seems like work when I collaborate with this team. Mowie Kay, I love working with you... simple as that. The way you transform a humble plate to look like a work of art always amazes me – you kind, gentle, lovely man. Lauren Miller – thank you for the wonderful props and for totally getting the vibe. Anna Hiddleston – you are a rock and a truly talented human – thank you for everything. My family the world over who are my true inspiration, and Matthew, my taste tester, number one food critic and partner in life – thank you x

FROM THE PUBLISHER

The publisher wishes to thank Jacqui Melville for the loan of some of the props and backgrounds for this book.